A CLASSIC RETELLING

hAMLET

by William Shakespeare

nextext

Cover photograph: Myron/stone
Photo research: Diane Hamilton.

Printed in Canada

ISBN-13: 978-0-618-12051-2
ISBN-10: 0-618-12051-3

5 6 7 8 9 NPC 09 08 07 06

Picture Acknowledgements
pages 13, 14, 18, 21–25: The Library of Congress.
pages 16, 29: from *The Complete Works of Shakespeare*, edited by David
          Bevington. Copyright © 1997 by Addison-Wesley Educational
          Publishers Inc. Reprinted by permission.
page 26: Corbis/Chris Heller.
page 27: The British Library.

Table of Contents

ACT ONE

On the walls of the castle at Elsinore in Denmark, two soldiers, Barnardo and Marcellus, wait with Horatio to question a ghost that appeared twice before. The ghost looks like the king of Denmark who died two months earlier and he refuses to speak. Horatio says he will tell his friend, Prince Hamlet, about the ghost.

While King Claudius drinks, Hamlet, Horatio,
and Marcellus see the ghost on the castle walls.
The ghost signals that Hamlet should follow it.
The others try to stop Hamlet, but he will not
allow them to hold him back. Hamlet goes off
with the ghost.

On another part of the castle wall, the ghost
says it is the spirit of Hamlet's father. The ghost
tells Hamlet that his father was murdered by his
uncle Claudius, who is now the king. The ghost
then tells Hamlet to revenge his murder. Hamlet
vows to carry out the revenge.

ACT TWO

In a room in Polonius's house, Polonius sends
his servant Reynaldo to spy on Laertes at school
in France. Ophelia tells Polonius that Hamlet
seems to have gone mad. Polonius decides that
Hamlet has gone mad because he loves
Ophelia, and she refuses to see him. He takes
Ophelia to see Claudius.

find the cause of Hamlet's madness. Polonius
arranges a meeting between Ophelia and
Hamlet. Polonius and King Claudius secretly
watch. When Ophelia tries to return his gifts,
suddenly turns on her and says he never loved
her. After Hamlet leaves, Claudius decides that
Hamlet's madness is not caused by love. He
says he will send Hamlet on a mission to
England. Polonius persuades the king to wait
until the queen has a chance to talk to Hamlet.

In a hall in Elsinore castle, Hamlet instructs the
actors. Then he asks Horatio to help him
watch King Claudius's reactions to the play. The
actors perform the play. Its story is very like
the murder of Hamlet's father, as told by the
ghost. When the actors are showing the murder,
King Claudius rushes out of the room. Hamlet
tells Horatio that this proves that the ghost is
telling the truth. Rosencrantz and Guildenstern
tell Hamlet that King Claudius is very angry and
that Queen Gertrude wants to speak to him
privately. Hamlet promises himself that he will
punish his mother only with words, not actions.

ACT FOUR

*will offer Hamlet some poisoned wine. Queen
Gertrude enters to tell them that Ophelia in her
madness has drowned.*

Hamlet is winning the fencing contest. Gertrude
drinks from the poisoned cup meant for
Hamlet. Laertes then wounds Hamlet with
the poisoned sword point. Hamlet grabs the
sword and wounds Laertes. Gertrude dies. Laertes,
dying from the poison, confesses the plot to
kill Hamlet. Hamlet kills King Claudius, but
before Hamlet dies, he asks Horatio to tell the
true story to everyone. He says Fortinbras will
be the next king of Denmark. After Hamlet
dies, Fortinbras arrives and restores order. He
orders a military funeral for Hamlet.

Vocabulary words appear in boldface type and are
footnoted. Specialized or technical words and phrases
appear in lightface type and are footnoted.

Background

William Shakespeare lived and wrote near the end of a time in European history known as the Renaissance, which lasted from 1485 to 1660. The word *renaissance* means "rebirth." During this exciting time, there was a rebirth of interest in the arts and sciences of the classical Greeks and Romans. Like many other writers of his time, Shakespeare used older works for his ideas. But he always gave them a different and more exciting twist.

The Story of *Hamlet*

Hamlet is one of the most puzzling of Shakespeare's plays. It is also the one most often performed. Hamlet, a Danish prince, meets a ghost that says it is his murdered father, the king of Denmark. The ghost tells him that his uncle, Claudius, killed his father and demands that

"I am your father's spirit, doomed!" says the ghost. He asks Hamlet for revenge.

▼

Hamlet take revenge. Then Hamlet seems to go mad. But is he really mad or just pretending? Why does he find it so hard to revenge his father's death? Why is Hamlet so cruel to Ophelia, the woman he is supposed to love? As you read the play, decide what you think really happened.

The story of Hamlet first appeared in Norse adventure stories. Then, in the twelfth century, the historian Saxo Grammaticus retold the story in his *Historiae Danicae*. It was probably first adapted for the English theater around 1580 by Thomas Kyd. Shakespeare rewrote the story in a completely different way. He focused on the confused inner life of Hamlet.

▲
A theater of Shakespeare's time.

Shakespeare's Theater

The Globe theater was built in 1599 in a small town outside London called Southwark. It was an outdoor summer theater. In 1613, the theater burned down. It was rebuilt in 1614 but was torn down in 1644. However, in London today, Shakespeare's plays are performed in a newly built Globe theater. Now, as it was in Shakespeare's time, when the flag is flying over the Globe, a play is going on.

The Globe theater was round and had no roof. Its stage stuck out into the audience. As many as 2,000 people attended the plays, and many of them stood on the ground around the stage. Three audience balconies had seats that were covered. The most expensive seats were on the shady side.

The stage had doors on either side. There was a small curtain-covered room at the back of the stage and two balconies above it. When *Hamlet* starts, the Danish soldiers are on the wall of the castle, which would have been the first balcony. The second balcony was for the musicians, whose music was like a soundtrack for the play. Several songs are sung in *Hamlet*, and trumpets are played frequently. Above the stage was a ceiling painted to look like the sky. It was held up by two columns. Above the ceiling was a special effects room. Cannons were fired there for battle scenes. Sound effects, like a howling wind, were also made in the special effects room. A large basket carrying actors could have been lowered from this room.

The stage also had a trap door. The ghost may have appeared and disappeared through it. In the play you will find stage directions, for example: [*They fight.*] These tell the actors what to do. Remember that you are reading a performance script. While the actors speak, they are also doing things, like crying, shouting, and fighting.

There were no lights in the theater. Plays were presented during the day. There was little scenery, although the stage was not completely empty. Scene changes were very fast, and there were beautiful costumes.

▲

Two gravediggers bring humor to this tragic play as they make jokes based on words that have more than one meaning.

Shakespeare's Language

Poetry

Shakespeare wrote his plays in verse. Some of it does not rhyme and some of it does. The meter, or rhythm of the language, is what makes it poetry. Shakespeare's poetry is in ten-syllable lines with alternating stresses. This kind of verse is called "iambic pentameter." For example, in Act Five, Scene Two, Horatio says:

> *Now cracks a noble heart. Good night, sweet prince,*
> *And flights of angels sing you to your rest!*

Most of the poetry in *Hamlet* does not rhyme, but it does have the rhythm of iambic pentameter. This is called "blank verse." When rhyme is used, it emphasizes some important idea. And, since his theater did not have lights or a curtain that came down, Shakespeare used two rhyming lines at the end of a scene to signal that the scene was over.

In this retelling, poetry is not used. However, some of Shakespeare's most famous lines have been included. A note will tell you when the lines are exactly as Shakespeare wrote them.

Imagery

A modern play or movie has scenery. In Shakespeare's time, there was very little scenery. So the characters had to describe the scene. Shakespeare wrote wonderful word pictures to present the images he wanted his audience to "see."

These images are not always beautiful. Sometimes the image is ugly. In Act Three, Scene Two, Hamlet speaks about midnight:

> *'Tis now the very witching time of night*
> *When churchyards yawn and hell itself breathes out*
> *Evil to this world.*

When Shakespeare wrote about a "witching time of night when churchyards yawn," he meant that the night is spooky and eerie. It is as if witches are coming out of hiding and the dead are coming out of their graves to wander around.

Puns and Other Fun with Words

Shakespeare loved to have fun with language. He and his audience liked words and phrases that have more than one meaning. Sometimes the wordplay would be a joke, and sometimes it would be used only for the surprise of the double meaning. In Act Two, Scene Two, Polonius is concerned for Hamlet's health. He asks Hamlet if he will "walk out of the air," meaning out of the unhealthy cold air. Hamlet asks if Polonius means he will walk into his grave. Which, as Polonius says, is indeed, "out of the air."

The ghost watches as Hamlet talks wildly to his mother, Queen Gertrude. ▶

The Characters

The Major Characters
Ghost

Claudius—brother of the dead King Hamlet, now king of Denmark

Hamlet—son of Queen Gertrude and the old King Hamlet, nephew to the present king

Gertrude—Hamlet's mother, wife of the dead King Hamlet; now wife of King Claudius

Members of the Court

Polonius—Lord Chamberlain of Denmark, the King's advisor

Laertes—Polonius's son

Ophelia—Polonius's daughter

Reynaldo—Polonius's servant

Voltemand and **Cornelius**—Danish ambassadors sent to Norway

Osric—a rich young man

Horatio—Hamlet's good friend

Rosencrantz and **Guildenstern**—Hamlet's school friends

▲
Ophelia

Minor Characters

Lords

Gentleman

Gravediggers

First Gravedigger

Second Gravedigger

Players (Actors)

First, Second, Third, Fourth Player—one gives the Prologue, the others play the King, the Queen, and Lucianus, the Poisoner

Soldiers

Fortinbras—Prince of Norway

Captain—a Norwegian in Fortinbras's army

Barnardo and Marcellus—officers in the Danish army

Francisco—a soldier in the Danish army

Others:

Priest

Messengers

Lords

Laertes's Followers

Musicians

Attendants

Soldiers

English Ambassador

Servant

Sailor

Hamlet comes in to kill the king, but finds him praying.
▼

The Plot

Hamlet is troubled by his father's death and his mother's marriage to his uncle, the new king.

▼

Act Three

King Claudius's reaction to the play proves his guilt to Hamlet. Hamlet has a chance to kill the king but lets it pass because King Claudius is praying. Later, Hamlet kills Polonius, thinking he is killing the king.

Act Two

In order to revenge his father's death, Hamlet pretends to be mad. The madness is blamed on his love for Ophelia. Hamlet decides to use a play to reveal the murder.

Act One

The ghost says it is Hamlet's father, the old king of Denmark. It tells Hamlet that the old king was murdered by Hamlet's uncle Claudius, the new king, who has married Hamlet's mother, Gertrude.

Climax

Rising Action

Beginning

Act Four

King Claudius sends Hamlet to England to be murdered. Ophelia goes mad. Hamlet returns to Denmark. King Claudius gets Laertes to help in a plan to kill Hamlet.

Falling Action

Act Five

The king's plan to murder Hamlet in a fencing match with Laertes works. Before he dies, Hamlet kills Laertes and the king. The queen dies from poison.

End

▲
William Shakespeare

Shakespeare's Life

Birth

Shakespeare was born in Stratford-upon-Avon, a small town about seventy-five miles northwest of London, England. His father, John Shakespeare, was a glove maker who owned a shop in Stratford and was elected to local government offices. Shakespeare's mother, Mary Arden, came from a well-off farming family. Shakespeare was baptized on April 26, 1564, a few days after his birth. He was the third of eight children.

Childhood

Shakespeare went to school in Stratford. At this time, most people did not get an education and could neither read nor write. His school day was nine hours long. Shakespeare's education gave him the background for much of his writing. In fact, he took many of his ideas for his history plays from a common schoolbook of the time, Holinshed's *Chronicles.*

Stratford was an excellent place in which to grow up. The town was surrounded by woods, fields, and farms. It was a market town where people came to buy and sell goods. It was very busy, and Shakespeare had a chance to meet and observe many different

▲
Stratford

types of people. During holidays, popular plays were performed. Traveling companies of actors visited the town, and there were two large fairs every year.

Marriage

In November 1582, at the age of eighteen, Shakespeare married Anne Hathaway, who was twenty-six. Their daughter Susanna was born in May 1583. Twins, Hamnet, a boy, and Judith, a girl, were born in 1585.

Queen Elizabeth I ▶

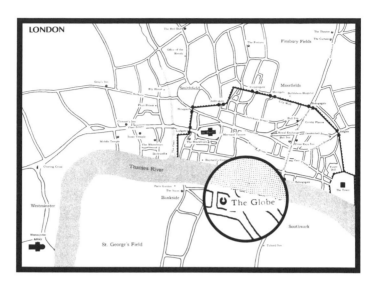

▲
Map of London

London

Seven years after the twins were born, Shakespeare was in London. He worked in the theaters—first in small jobs, then as an actor, and finally as a writer of plays. In 1599, he and six others became owners of the new Globe theater. Queen Elizabeth I supported Shakespeare's company. James I, who became king in 1603, gave the company a royal license. After that, it was known as the King's Men. The company often presented plays for the royal court.

Writing

Shakespeare's first plays were like those of another very popular author, Christopher Marlowe. As Shakespeare wrote more, he developed his own style. He wrote thirty-seven plays in all. His success came in part because he knew firsthand how audiences behaved and what they wanted. He gave audiences exciting stories. He provided funny moments in the middle of tragedies and tragic moments in the middle of comedies. He knew how easily audiences got bored and restless. He made sure there were surprises, magic events, songs, fights, love scenes, and jokes in all his plays.

The years 1592 to 1594 were times of great sickness and disease. The bubonic plague hit London then, and the theaters were often closed. Shakespeare turned to writing poems. He wrote two long, storytelling poems based on Roman mythology, *Venus and Adonis* (1593) and *The Rape of Lucrece* (1594). He also wrote a collection of 154 of the fourteen-line poems known as sonnets.

Later Years

Shakespeare's work brought him fame and money. In 1597, he bought himself a very large house called New Place in Stratford. He moved into it in 1610, and began to spend more and more time there. His last play was *The Tempest,* in which a magician who has lived on a deserted magical island returns to his own land after he breaks his magical staff. Shakespeare seems to have gone on helping to write and fix other people's plays after he stopped writing his own. He died in 1616 and was buried in the church at Stratford.

▲
This is what New Place probably looked like during Shakespeare's ownership.

A Shakespeare Time Line

1564—William Shakespeare is baptized on April 26.

1582—He gets a license to marry Anne Hathaway in November.

1592—He is living in London. His first plays have been performed.

1592–1594—The bubonic plague spreads to London. Theaters close. Shakespeare turns to writing poetry.

1599—Shakespeare and six others buy the Globe theater.

1603—Queen Elizabeth I dies. The king of Scotland becomes James I, king of England. *Hamlet* is first published.

1610—Shakespeare writes his last play, *The Tempest*.

1616—William Shakespeare dies on April 23.

act one

On the walls of the castle at Elsinore in Denmark, two soldiers, Barnardo and Marcellus, wait with Horatio to question a ghost that appeared twice before. The ghost looks like the king of Denmark who died two months earlier and he refuses to speak. Horatio says he will tell his friend, Prince Hamlet, about the ghost.

[Francisco *is on guard.* Barnardo *enters.*]

Barnardo. Who's there?

Francisco. No, you answer me. Stand and give your name.

Barnardo. Long live the king!

Francisco. Barnardo?

Barnardo. Yes.

Francisco. You are right on time.

Barnardo. It's just now midnight. Go to bed, Francisco.

Francisco. I'm glad you're here. It's bitter cold, and I'm tired.

Barnardo. Have you had a quiet guard?[1]

Francisco. Not a mouse stirring.

Barnardo. Well, good night. If you meet Horatio and Marcellus, who are also on duty, tell them to hurry.

Francisco. I think I hear them. Stop! Who's there?

[*Enter* Horatio *and* Marcellus.]

Horatio. Friends to Denmark.

Marcellus. And loyal followers of the king.

Francisco. May God give you a good night.

Marcellus. O, good night, honest soldier. Who has taken your place?

Francisco. Barnardo. Good night.

[Francisco *exits.*]

Marcellus. Holla![2] Barnardo!

---

[1] guard—these soldiers are on guard duty. They walk around the castle walls to keep out enemies.

[2] Holla—*Hola* is the Spanish word for "hello," frequently used in Shakespeare's England.

Barnardo. Is Horatio there?

Horatio. A piece of him.[3]

Barnardo. Welcome, Horatio. Welcome, good Marcellus.

Marcellus. Has this thing appeared again tonight?

Barnardo. I haven't seen anything.

Marcellus. Horatio says it's our imagination. He will not believe what we have seen twice. So I've begged him to watch with us tonight. If this **apparition**[4] comes again, he may see it and speak to it.

Horatio. Nonsense! It won't appear.

Barnardo. Sit down for a while, and let us tell you once more what we have seen two nights in a row.

Horatio. Well, tell me, Barnardo.

Barnardo. Last night at one o'clock, Marcellus and I—

[*Enter the* Ghost.]

Marcellus. Peace! Look, it comes again!

---

[3] Perhaps because it's so late, Horatio doesn't feel he is completely there, not fully awake.

[4] **apparition**—something that isn't there; a ghost.

Barnardo. In the same shape, like the dead king.

Marcellus. You are a **scholar**.[5] Speak to it, Horatio.

Barnardo. Doesn't it look like the king? Look at it, Horatio.

Horatio. It looks very much like him. It fills me with fear and wonder.

Barnardo. It wants us to speak to it.

Marcellus. Speak to it, Horatio.

Horatio. What are you that comes so late looking like the handsome soldier, the dead king of Denmark? By heaven, I command you, speak!

Marcellus. It is insulted.

Barnardo. See, it **stalks**[6] away!

Horatio. Stop! Speak, speak! I command you, speak!

[*Exit the* Ghost.]

Marcellus. It's gone and will not answer.

Barnardo. How are you now, Horatio! You tremble and look pale. Isn't this more than imagination? What do you think about it?

---

[5] **scholar**—learned person; well educated person.

[6] **stalks**—walks stiffly and proudly.

Horatio. Before my God, I would not believe this if I hadn't seen it with my own eyes.

Marcellus. Doesn't it look like the king?

Horatio. As you look like yourself. That was the armor he had on when he fought the king of Norway. That's how he frowned when he conquered the Polish army. It's strange.

Marcellus. Twice before, and exactly at this dead hour, like a marching soldier he has gone by our watch post.

Horatio. I don't know what this means. In my opinion, there is some terrible trouble in our kingdom.

Marcellus. Enough of that for now. Please, sit down. Does anyone know why the people are being worked night and day so hard to prepare for war? Do you know?

Horatio. I do. At least, I know the rumor. Our last king, who just now seemed to be here, was challenged by King Fortinbras of Norway. Our king killed the old King Fortinbras in combat. They fought over land that they owned themselves, not their kingdoms. With the death of Fortinbras, our king gained Fortinbras's land. Now, sir, Fortinbras's young son has raised an outlaw army, and it looks like he is going to try to get back by force the land his father lost. I believe this is why there is so much quick preparation for war.

Barnardo. I think you're right. This may be why this frightful figure who appears as our dead king comes armed here night after night. He was and is the cause of these wars.

Horatio. When Rome ruled the world,
Right before the mighty Julius[7] fell,
The graves opened, and the dead walked and
wailed in the Roman streets.
Stars fell from the sky. The dew was bloody.
The sun showed signs of disasters, and the
moon almost disappeared.
These same signs have been seen
Here in our own country right before disasters.
But wait a minute, look! It comes again!

[*Enter the* Ghost.]

I'll question it, though it blast me. Stop, **illusion!**[8]
If you can speak, speak to me.
If any good thing can be done
That may help you and give a blessing to me,
Speak to me.

---

[7] Julius Caesar was the first Caesar, or ruler, of Rome. Shakespeare wrote about Julius Caesar's death in another play.

[8] **illusion**—something that isn't really there; a dream, a vision.

[*A rooster crows.*[9]]

    If you know something about our country's
        future
    And can help us with the knowledge,
    O, speak!
    Or if you have buried treasure in your life,
    Stolen treasure, for which, they say, you spirits
        often walk in death,
    Speak of it.

[*The* Ghost *starts to leave.*]

    Stop, and speak! Stop it, Marcellus.

Marcellus. Shall I strike at it with my spear?

Horatio. Yes, if it will not stop.

Barnardo. It's here!

Horatio. It's here!

[*The* Ghost *exits.*]

Marcellus. It's gone! Since it is so much like the old
    king, we shouldn't try to hurt it. For it is like the
    air. It cannot be hurt. Our blows are useless.

Barnardo. It was about to speak when the
    rooster crowed.

---

[9] Roosters crow at the first light of day. This is a signal that night is over. The ghost can't stay any longer.

Horatio. And then it jumped like a guilty person. I have heard it said that the rooster's crow in the morning calls the wandering spirit to his prison. This spirit's actions seem to prove this.

Marcellus. It faded when the rooster crowed. Some say that when Christmas is celebrated, the rooster, the bird of dawn, sings all night long. And then, they say, no spirit dares to walk. The nights are pure. Then nothing evil happens. No fairy can cast a spell. No witch can make a charm, so holy and so good is the time.[10]

Horatio. So I have heard, and I partly believe it. But, look, it is morning. This is the end of our watch. Let's tell young Hamlet[11] what we have seen tonight. I think this spirit, which will not speak to us, will speak to him. Do you agree that we should tell Hamlet about it? He's our friend, and it is our duty.

Marcellus. Let's do it. I know where we will find Hamlet this morning.

[*They exit.*]

---

[10] This Christmas legend is found only in Shakespeare.
[11] young Hamlet—the dead king's son. Both father and son are named Hamlet.

In a hall in Elsinore castle, King Claudius, Hamlet's uncle and the new king, sends ambassadors to Norway. He tells them to stop an attack from Fortinbras, a prince of Norway. King Claudius blames Hamlet for grieving too much over his father's death. He tells Hamlet that he should not return to his university. When Hamlet is left alone, he says he is upset because his mother married his uncle so quickly after his father died. When he hears about the ghost, Hamlet says he will watch for it that night.

[*Enter* King Claudius, Queen Gertrude, Hamlet, Polonius, Laertes, Voltemand, Cornelius, Lords, *and* Attendants.]

King Claudius. Because my brother and your
     king has lately died,
  Our hearts are full of grief, and our whole
     kingdom

Is filled with sorrow. We[1] have had to think
   of him and of ourselves as well.
Therefore our once sister-in-law and now
   our queen,
Equally with delight and sadness, we have
   married
Joining ourselves to this kingship. You have all
Agreed to this marriage. To all, our thanks.
Now for the reason we have called this meeting.
Here is the business. Young Fortinbras, thinking
   us weak
And overcome by our late dear brother's death,
Pesters us with demands that we surrender
   lands lost by his father.
We have written to the king of Norway,
   uncle of young Fortinbras.[2]
The king is sick and does not leave his bed.
He does not hear of his nephew's plans.
Voltemand and Cornelius, we send you
To tell the old king that his nephew is forming
   an army of his people
And raising money to attack us. [*He gives them
   a paper.*] Farewell, and go swiftly.

---

[1] Kings often refer to themselves as "we" because they represent the whole kingdom. This use is called "the royal plural."

[2] The situation in Norway is just like what is happening in Denmark. The son has not inherited the kingship. The old king's brother has become king.

Cornelius and **Voltemand.** In that and all things we will do our duty.

King Claudius. We do not doubt it. Heartily farewell. [*Exit* Voltemand *and* Cornelius.] And now, Laertes, how are you? You said there was something you want. If it is reasonable, you won't waste your breath. What is there, Laertes, that I wouldn't give you without your asking? The head is not more connected to the heart, the hand more important to the mouth, than is the throne of Denmark to your father Polonius. What do you want, Laertes?

Laertes. My dread[3] Lord, I wish you to allow me to return to France; from where I willingly came to Denmark to show my support for your **coronation**.[4] Yet now, I must confess, since my duty is done, my thoughts and wishes turn again to France. I wait only for your permission to go back.

King Claudius. Do you have your father's permission? What does Polonius say?

---

[3] dread—powerful; to be feared. This is a respectful greeting for the king. It is also true that Claudius is to be feared.

[4] **coronation**—being crowned king.

Polonius. My Lord, he has worked hard to get my permission, and at last I agreed. I beg you, let him go.

King Claudius. You may spend your time as you wish, Laertes. But now, my cousin[5] Hamlet, and my son—

Hamlet. [*Aside*][6] A little more than kin, and less than kind.[7]

King Claudius. How is it that the clouds[8] still hang on you?

Hamlet. That's not so, my lord. I am too much in the sun.[9]

Queen Gertrude. Good Hamlet, throw off your black mourning clothes. Let everyone see you are happy here. Do not always look down, seeking your noble father in the dust. You know that death happens to everyone. All that lives must die, passing through nature to the hereafter.

---

[5] cousin—was used to name any relative, except a brother. It was also used to address friends. Hamlet is actually Claudius's nephew.

[6] In an aside, the actor speaks to the audience. The rest of the actors onstage are not supposed to be able to hear this.

[7] more than kin, and less than kind—*Wordplay:* They are doubly related. Since Claudius has married Hamlet's mother, he is Hamlet's uncle and (step) father. But Hamlet does not feel "kindly" toward Claudius. They are not the same "kind"—family or type.

[8] clouds—sorrows. Hamlet is wearing the black clothes usually worn by mourners.

[9] People are too cheerful, considering Hamlet's father has only been dead a short time. Or, Hamlet is too much his father's "son" not to show his sorrow.

Hamlet. Yes, madam, it is common.

Queen Gertrude. If it is so, why do you seem to take this so personally?

Hamlet. "Seem," madam! No, it *is*. I do not know "seem." It's not only my dark cloak, good mother, nor my suits of solemn black, nor forced sighs. No, it is not all the tears my eyes have shed. It is not the sad look of my face, together with all the other forms, methods, shapes of grief, that can show what I feel. These indeed "seem," for a man might pretend to do these things. But I have that in me which is greater than I can show. These are just the outward signs of sorrow.

King Claudius. It is sweet and right of you, Hamlet,
To be sad for your father.
But you must know, your father lost a father.
That lost father lost his father, and each son
    was bound
By duty to mourn for his lost father for
    some time,
But to keep mourning shows **impious**[10]
    stubbornness. It is unmanly grief.
It shows that you wish to go against
    God's wishes.

---

[10] **impious**—going against God or your religion.

It shows a heart without religion, an
    impatient mind, a simple and unschooled
    understanding.
We know death must come for everyone.
Why should we believe it hurts only us?
Fie! It is a sin against God, a sin against
    the dead,
A sin against nature, to think this foolish way.
Fathers die before sons.
From the first death till he that died today,
People have said "This must be so." We beg
    you, let go
Of this useless sorrow, and think of us
As your father. Let everyone hear,
You are the next in line to get our throne.
I love you as much as any father loves his son.
As for your plan to go back to school in
    Wittenberg,[11]
It is very much against our wishes. We beg
    you, force yourself to stay
Here in the cheer and comfort of our presence,
As our chief courtier, cousin, and our son.

Queen Gertrude. Let not your mother's prayers
be lost, Hamlet. I pray you, stay with us. Do not
go to Wittenberg.

---

[11] Wittenberg was a famous university in Germany.

Hamlet. I shall do my best to obey you, madam.[12]

King Claudius. Why, that is a loving and a
    good reply.
Be as ourself in Denmark.—Madam, come.
This gentle and willing agreement of Hamlet
    makes my heart happy.
And as a sign of thanks, whenever I drink
    a health to anyone today,
The cannon shall be fired. Come, let's leave.

[*Exit all but* Hamlet.]

Hamlet. O, that this too, too sullied[13] flesh
    would melt,
Thaw, and turn itself into a dew![14]
Or that God had not made
His laws against suicide! O God! God!
How weary, stale, flat, and unprofitable,
Seem to me all the uses of this world!
Fie on it! Ah fie! The world is a weed-
    filled garden.
Only stinking things that are gross in nature
Are in it. That it should come to this!
My father is only two months dead.
No, not even that much, not two.

---

[12] Hamlet answers his mother's request, not the king's.

[13] sullied—stained; impure; imperfect. Often written as *solid*.

[14] Hamlet wishes to disappear like ice melting.

He was so excellent a king that, compared to
    this new king,
He was a glorious god compared to a drunken
    half-human beast.
He was so loving to my mother
That he would not allow the winds
To visit her face too roughly. Heaven and earth!
Must I remember? Why, she would hang on him
As if her appetite had grown
By what it fed on. And yet, within a month
(Let me not think about it—**frailty**,[15] your
    name is woman!)
A little month, before those shoes were old
With which she followed my poor father's
    body to the grave,
Like Niobe,[16] all tears—why she, even she
(O, God! A beast, that can't even reason, would
    have mourned longer)
She married my uncle, my father's brother,
But no more like my father than I am like
    Hercules.[17]
Within a month, before the salt of her false tears
Had stopped turning her eyes red, she married.

---

[15] **frailty**—weakness.

[16] Niobe, in Greek mythology, is a symbol of extreme sorrow. She cried over
the death of her children until she was turned into a fountain.

[17] Hercules, in Greek mythology, was the strongest man alive.

O, most wicked speed, to rush
So quickly to incestuous[18] sheets!
It is not, nor it cannot become good.
But break, my heart; for I must not speak.

[*Enter* Horatio, Marcellus, *and* Barnardo.]

Horatio. Hail to your lordship!

Hamlet. I am glad to see you well. Horatio? It is
you, Horatio, isn't it?

Horatio. Yes, my lord, and your poor servant ever.

Hamlet. Sir, my good friend. You are my friend,
not my servant. And why have you left
Wittenberg, Horatio? Marcellus?

Marcellus. My good lord.

Hamlet. I am very glad to see you. [*To* Barnardo]
Good evening, sir. [*To* Horatio] But why have
you left Wittenberg?

Horatio. I felt like being a truant,[19] my lord.

Hamlet. I would not hear your enemy say so, nor
shall you make me believe anything bad about

---

[18] incestuous—concerning having sex with someone who is too closely related.
Marrying one's dead brother's wife was considered incest and adultery.

[19] a truant—someone absent without permission.

you. I know you are no truant. But why are you in Elsinore? We'll teach you to drink deep before you leave.

Horatio. My lord, I came to see your father's funeral.

Hamlet. I beg you, do not **mock**[20] me, fellow student. I think it was to see my mother's wedding.

Horatio. Indeed, my lord, it came very quickly afterwards.

Hamlet. Thrift,[21] thrift, Horatio! The left-over baked meats for the funeral were the cold cuts for the marriage tables. I would have rather met my worst enemy in heaven before I had seen that day, Horatio! My father!—I think I see my father.[22]

Horatio. Where, my lord?

Hamlet. In my mind's eye, Horatio.

Horatio. I saw him once. He was an excellent king.

---

[20] **mock**—make fun of.

[21] **Thrift**—careful money management. Hamlet is being sarcastic.

[22] This startles Horatio because he did see Hamlet's father, the ghost.

Hamlet. He was a man. Remembering him, I think
I shall not look upon as good a man again.

Horatio. My lord, I think I saw him last night.

Hamlet. Saw? Who?

Horatio. My lord, the king your father.

Hamlet. The king my father!

Horatio. Control your surprise for a while. Listen
to what I have to say and the marvel these
gentlemen saw.

Hamlet. For God's love, let me hear!

Horatio. For two nights have these gentlemen,
Marcellus and Barnardo, on their watch,
In the dead middle of the night,
Met a figure that looked like your father,
Armed at every point from head to foot.
It appeared before them, and marched slowly
   by them.
Three times it walked by their fearful eyes,
Within an arm's length, while they,
Turned almost to jelly with fear,
Couldn't speak to it. They secretly
Told me about this, and I went with them the
   third night.

Then, as they had reported, at the time they said,
The ghost came. I knew your father.
My hands are not more like each other
Than this ghost was like your father.

Hamlet. But where was this?

Marcellus. My lord, on the castle walls where we watched.

Hamlet. Did you speak to it?

Horatio. My lord, I did.
It didn't answer. Yet once I thought it lifted up
   its head
And looked like it would speak. But even then
The morning rooster crowed loudly,
And at the sound the ghost quickly shrank away
And was gone from our sight.

Hamlet. It's very strange.

Horatio. As I do live, my honored lord, it's true.
And we thought it our duty to tell you.

Hamlet. Indeed, sirs, but this troubles me. Are you on guard duty tonight?

Marcellus and **Barnardo.** We are, my lord.

Hamlet. The ghost was armed, you say?

Marcellus. Armed, my lord.

Hamlet. Armed from head to toe?

Barnardo. My lord, from head to foot.

Hamlet. Then you didn't see his face?

Horatio. O, yes, my lord. He wore the face guard of his helmet up.

Hamlet. Did he look angry?

Horatio. More sad than angry.

Hamlet. Was he pale or red?

Horatio. Very pale.

Hamlet. Did he fix his eyes on you?

Horatio. All the time.

Hamlet. I wish I had been there.

Horatio. It would have much amazed you.

Hamlet. Very likely. Did it stay long?

Horatio. About as long as it takes to count to one hundred slowly.

Marcellus. Longer, longer.

Horatio. Not when I saw it.

Hamlet. His beard was gray—no?

Horatio. It looked like it did when I last saw him—silver.

Hamlet. I will watch tonight. Perhaps it will walk again.

Horatio. I am sure it will.

Hamlet. If it looks like my noble father,
I'll speak to it, even if hell itself should open
And tell me to be quiet. I pray you all,
If you have up to now not told anyone
    about this,
Keep it a secret. And whatever else shall
    happen tonight,
Think about it, but do not speak about it.
I will reward your friendship. So, fare you well.
I'll visit you on the wall between eleven
    and twelve.

All. We will obey your honor.

Hamlet. My friends, farewell. [*All but* Hamlet *exit.*] My father's spirit in armor! All is not well. Something is wrong. I wish the night would come quickly! Until then, be still, my soul. Evil acts will be discovered, even if all the Earth tries to hide them from men's eyes.

[Hamlet *exits.*]

In a room in Polonius's house, Laertes says goodbye to his sister Ophelia and warns her not to trust Hamlet's promises of love. Their father, Polonius, joins them. He gives Laertes much advice. After Laertes leaves, Polonius questions Ophelia. He then tells her that she should not see Hamlet again.

[*Enter* Laertes *and his sister* Ophelia.]

Laertes. My bags have been put on the ship. Farewell. And, sister, send me a letter when you can.

Ophelia. Do you think I'll forget?

Laertes. As for Hamlet and his youthful love for you, it is a passing flirtation, a violet in the spring of his nature. Early, not permanent. Sweet, not lasting. The perfume and game of a minute. No more.

Ophelia. No more?

Laertes. No more. For as a man grows in age, he also grows in thoughts. Hamlet will have important matters to think about. Perhaps he loves you now. Now he isn't trying to deceive you. But you must be afraid. He is an important man. He cannot always do what he would like to do. He may not choose a wife for himself, as less important men do. The safety and health of the country depend on him. His choice must always be what is best for his country. If he says he loves you, it is wise to believe it only as much as he can do what he wishes. He cannot do any more than his position will allow him to do. Think what loss your reputation may suffer if you believe everything he says in his love songs, or if you lose your heart, or your virginity, when he asks for it. Fear it, Ophelia, fear it, my dear sister. Keep your love out of danger. The most careful young girl is not careful enough if she shows her beauty in the moonlight.[1] People will gossip even when there is nothing to gossip about. The worms injure the young spring flowers too often before they have a chance to

---

[1] Laertes is quoting sayings that were very common in Shakespeare's time. He is giving his sister advice in much the same way that his father later on will give him advice.

bloom. And great dangers lie in the morning dew of youth. Be careful. You are safest if you are afraid. Youth finds it too easy to lose self-control, even without being tempted.

Ophelia. I shall remember this good lesson. But, my brother, do not, as some ungodly preachers do, show me how to live a good and pure life while you walk the primrose path[2] of self-indulgence and do not take your own advice.

Laertes. O, don't worry about me. I have stayed too long. Here comes our father.
[*Enter* Polonius.]
To receive a father's blessing twice is a double grace.[3] The time smiles upon a second goodbye.

Polonius. Still here, Laertes! Aboard, get aboard your ship. For shame!
The wind fills your ship's sail, and they wait
    for you.
[Polonius *blesses* Laertes, *perhaps with a hug or kiss.*]
There! My blessing go with you!
And keep these few thoughts in your memory:
Don't speak without thinking.
Don't act on any wild thought.
Be friendly, but by no means too friendly.

---

[2] primrose path—the tempting and easy way, which leads to hell.

[3] grace—favor from heaven.

Fix your true friends to your soul with bands
    of steel,
But do not try to entertain every spirited
    young man you meet.
Beware of entering a quarrel, but when you're
    in one,
Fight hard so that the person you quarrel with
    may beware of you.
Give every man your ear, but few your voice.
Listen to every man's criticism, but hold back
    your own.
Let your clothes be as good as you can buy,
But not fancy: rich, not wild.
For the clothes often tell about the man.
In France, the best people are very careful
And show their fine taste in the way they
    choose their clothes.
Neither a borrower nor a lender be.
For loans are often lost, and so are friends
    who lend,
And borrowing leaves you in debt.
This above all: to thine own self be true,
And it must follow, as the night follows the day,
Thou canst not then be false to any man.[4]
Farewell. My blessing goes with this advice!

---

[4] The previous three lines are as Shakespeare wrote them. They are very
famous and often quoted. They mean that if you are true to yourself, you
cannot be false to anyone else.

Laertes. I take my leave most humbly, my lord.

Polonius. It is time. Go, your servants are waiting.

Laertes. Farewell, Ophelia. Remember well what I have said to you.

Ophelia. It is locked in my memory. And you shall keep the key to it.

Laertes. Farewell.

[Laertes *exits.*]

Polonius. Ophelia, what did he say to you?

Ophelia. So please you, something about Lord Hamlet.

Polonius. Marry,[5] I'm glad you reminded me. I have been told that lately Hamlet has often spent much time alone with you. You have paid much attention to him. If this is true, as it was told to me, I must tell you something. You do not understand yourself as much as is right for my daughter and your honor. What is between you? Tell me the truth.

Ophelia. He has, my lord, lately made many tenders[6] of his affection for me.

---

[5] Marry—an expression similar to *indeed.* It could show surprise, agreement, or indignation.

[6] tenders—offers. See how Polonius plays with this word.

Polonius. Affection! Pooh! You speak like a green[7] girl. You are inexperienced in such dangerous dealings. Do you believe his "tenders," as you call them?

Ophelia. I do not know what I should think, my lord.

Polonius. Marry, I'll teach you. Think yourself a baby that you have taken these tenders, which are not real, for true money. Tender[8] yourself at a higher rate, or you'll tender me a fool.

Ophelia. My Lord, he has often begged me to accept his love in an honorable fashion.

Polonius. Ay, "fashion" you may call it. I don't believe it.

Ophelia. He has supported the truth of his speech, my lord, with almost all the holy vows of heaven.

Polonius. Yes, traps to catch stupid little birds. I do know
That when the blood burns, the soul

---

[7] green—young and inexperienced.

[8] *Wordplay*: *Tender* here means "regard"; "you'll tender me a fool," could mean "you'll show yourself to be a fool," or "make me look like a fool," or "give me a grandchild."

Lets the tongue make false promises. These love
    fires, daughter, give more light than heat.
They burn up all promises as they are
    being made.
You must not take them for real fire.
From now on be more careful how you spend
    your time.
Make it more difficult for him to talk to you.
As for Lord Hamlet,
Believe only that he is young,
And that he has more freedom than you have.
Briefly, Ophelia, do not believe his promises,
For they are not what they appear to be.
His promises are not unholy, but they will try
    to lead you
To something unholy. They seem like holy
    promises,
So they can trick you. This is all I have to say.
In plain terms, from now on
I do not want you to waste any of your free
    time talking to Lord Hamlet.
Pay attention. This is my command. Come
    along now.

Ophelia. I shall obey, my lord.

[*They exit.*]

ACT ONE, SCENE FOUR

While King Claudius drinks, Hamlet, Horatio, and Marcellus see the ghost on the castle walls. The ghost signals that Hamlet should follow it. The others try to stop Hamlet, but he will not allow them to hold him back. Hamlet goes off with the ghost.

[*Enter* Hamlet, Horatio, *and* Marcellus.]

Hamlet. The wind is sharp. It is very cold.

Horatio. It is a biting wind.

Hamlet. What time is it now?

Horatio. I think it's almost twelve.

Hamlet. No, it has struck twelve.

Horatio. Indeed? I didn't hear the bell. Then it's near the time when the spirit usually walks.
[*The sound of trumpets and cannon shots, offstage.*]
What does this mean, my lord?

Hamlet. The king is staying awake and drinking tonight. He drinks to everyone and dances drunkenly. And, as he drains his glasses of wine, the kettledrum and trumpet shout out the triumph of his drinking.

Horatio. Is it a custom?

Hamlet. Ay, marry, it is.
But, to my mind, though I am native here
And to the manner born, it is a custom
More honored in the breach than the observance.[1]
This heavy drinking makes us blamed by
    other nations.
They call us drunkards and pigs and hurt our
    reputation.[2]
And indeed it takes away from our good deeds.
Even a small amount of evil makes something
    admirable seem bad.

[*Enter the* Ghost.]

Horatio. Look, my lord, it comes!

Hamlet. Angels and ministers of grace defend us!
[*Speaking to the* Ghost]

---

[1] Although Hamlet has to accept this custom because he was born a prince, he thinks it would be better if it were not observed. These three lines are in Shakespeare's words.

[2] **reputation**—good name, the way others see our character.

Are you a good spirit or a goblin damned?[3]

Do you bring airs from heaven or blasts
  from hell?

Whether your plans are wicked or good,

You come in such a questionable shape

That I must speak to you. I'll call you "Hamlet,"[4]

"King," "Father," "Royal Dane." O, answer me!

Let me not burst in ignorance, but tell

Why your bones put in the earth in a
  Christian burial

Have burst out of the grave? Why has the
  sepulcher,[5]

Where we saw you quietly placed,

Opened his heavy marble jaws,

To throw you out again? What does this mean,

That you, dead body, visit the night again,

Making us shake in fear with thoughts that
  even our souls

Can't understand? What are you doing?

What should we do?

[*The* Ghost *beckons* Hamlet.[6]]

---

[3] This was a very important question to Hamlet and to Shakespeare's audience. Is this really the ghost of Hamlet's father, or is this an evil spirit, a demon, sent to get Hamlet in trouble?

[4] Hamlet's father was also named Hamlet.

[5] sepulcher—tomb; burial building. In the next lines the tomb is described as if it were a person or animal.

[6] *beckons* Hamlet—motions Hamlet to come to it.

Horatio. It beckons you to come away with it, as if it wished to speak to you alone.

Marcellus. Look how politely it waves you to go with it. But do not go with it.

Horatio. No, by no means.

Hamlet. It will not speak here, so I will follow it.

Horatio. Do not go, my lord.

Hamlet. Why should I be afraid? My life is not worth a pin. And for my soul, what can the ghost do to that? My soul is as **immortal**[7] as any ghost. It waves to me again. I'll follow it.

Horatio. What if it tempts you toward the ocean, my lord, or to the dreadful top of the cliff that hangs over the sea, and there takes some other horrible form, which might drive you mad? Think of it. The very place puts thoughts of suicide in men's heads, without real reasons except that they look so far down to the sea and hear it roar below them.

Hamlet. It still waves at me. [*To the* Ghost] Go on. I'll follow you.

---

[7] **immortal**—lasting forever; undying.

Marcellus. You shall not go, my lord. [*They try to hold* Hamlet *back.*]

Hamlet. Take your hands off me.

Horatio. Do what we say. You shall not go.

Hamlet. My fate cries out, and makes me as strong as the Nemean lion.[8] Still I am called. Let me go, gentlemen. [Hamlet *breaks free and draws his sword.*] By heaven, I'll make a ghost of anyone that tries to stop me! I say, get away! [*To the* Ghost] Go on. I'll follow you.

[*The* Ghost *and* Hamlet *exit.*]

Horatio. He is desperate.

Marcellus. Let's follow. It's not right to obey him when he is like this.

Horatio. Let's go. What does all this mean?

Marcellus. Something is rotten in the state of Denmark.

Horatio. God will take care of it.

Marcellus. No, let's follow him.

[*They exit.*]

---

[8] Nemean lion—in Greek mythology, a lion that Hercules had to fight.

On another part of the castle wall, the ghost says it is the
spirit of Hamlet's father. The ghost tells Hamlet that his
father was murdered by his uncle Claudius, who is now
the king. The ghost then tells Hamlet to revenge his murder.
Hamlet vows to carry out the revenge.

[*Enter the* Ghost *and* Hamlet.]

Hamlet. Where will you lead me? Speak! I'll go
no farther.

Ghost. Hear me.

Hamlet. I will.

Ghost. The time is almost come when I must
return to sulphurous and torturing fire.[1]

Hamlet. Alas, poor ghost!

---

[1] The fires of hell were thought to smell like sulfur (also spelled *sulphur*).

Ghost. Don't pity me. Pay close attention to what
   I shall say.

Hamlet. Speak. I must hear.

Ghost. So must you **revenge** me[2] when you
   hear me.

Hamlet. What?

Ghost. I am your father's spirit,
   Doomed for a certain time to walk the night
   And, for the day, made to suffer in fires
   Until the evil sins I did when I lived
   Are burned and cleaned away. I am forbidden
   To tell the secrets of my prison house,
   Or I could tell a story whose smallest word
   Would torture your soul, freeze your
      young blood,
   Make your two eyes, like shooting stars,
      jump from their places.
   It would make each hair on your head stand
      on end.
   But this story of the afterlife must not be
   Told to living ears. Listen, listen, O, listen!
   If you ever loved your dear father—

Hamlet. O God!

---

[2] **revenge** me—punish the person who did this injury to me.

Ghost. Revenge my evil and most unnatural murder.

Hamlet. Murder!

Ghost. Murder most **foul**,[3] as all murder is.
But this murder was most evil, strange, and
unnatural.

Hamlet. Tell me quickly, so that I may rush to my
revenge with wings as swift as thought.[4]

Ghost. I find you well suited to this task. Now,
Hamlet, hear me.
It was said that while I was sleeping in my
orchard,
A snake bit me and I died. Everyone in
Denmark
Is completely misled by this lie. But know,
noble youth,
The snake that took your father's life
Now wears his crown.

Hamlet. O my **prophetic**[5] soul! My uncle!

Ghost. Yes, that incestuous, that adulterous beast,
With the witchcraft of his wit,[6] with evil gifts—

---

[3] **foul**—evil.

[4] Hamlet says he will rush to revenge his father's murder, but the problem in
the play is that he doesn't rush.

[5] **prophetic**—able to know the truth before it happens.

[6] **wit**—cleverness. Today *wit* usually means "humor." In the past it was a more
complicated word. It really meant "the ability to see more clearly and quickly."

O wicked wit and gifts, that have the power
To deceive people!—He won the love
Of my most virtuous-seeming queen.
O Hamlet, to lose me, a man who loved her
  with all the true vows of marriage,
And go to him, that beast. But, quiet!
I think I smell the morning air.[7]
Let me be brief. I was sleeping in my orchard,
As I always did in the afternoon,
When your uncle crept in with a small bottle
  of poison.
He poured it in my ear. It quickly
Flowed through my body
And covered me with vile and ugly scabs.
In this way, I was sleeping and my brother's
  hand
Took my life, my crown, my queen at once.
I was killed without time for confession and
  the last rites of the Christian church.[8]
All my sins were unforgiven.
O, horrible! O, horrible, most horrible!
If you have any feelings for me, do something.
Do not let the royal bed of Denmark be
A couch for lust and damned incest.

---

[7] The ghost cannot stay after the sun rises.

[8] Hamlet's father couldn't confess his sins and have them forgiven, so he must suffer for them after death.

But, whatever you do about this,
Do not let your mind or your soul
Plan to harm your mother. Leave it to heaven
And to her own guilty conscience to wound
    and sting her.
Farewell now. Morning is near.
Adieu, adieu![9] Hamlet, remember me.

[*The* Ghost *exits.*]

Hamlet. O all you angels in heaven! O Earth!
What is happening?
What if this spirit was from hell?[10] O, fie!
    Peace, peace, my heart.
And you, my muscles, don't grow instantly old,
But hold me bravely up.
Remember you?
Yes, you poor ghost, while I have any memory
In this confusing world.
Remember you?
Yes. I'll forget all small and foolish memories,
All quotations from books, all ideas, all
    impressions from the past,
All that my youthful mind wrote there.
Only your commandment shall live

---

[9] adieu—French for "goodbye."

[10] Hamlet worries that this may not be the real ghost of his father. It may be a false ghost sent by the devil to try to get him to do something evil.

Within the book and volume of my brain. Yes,
   by heaven!
O most destructive woman![11]
O **villain**,[12] villain, smiling, damned villain!
My notebook—I should write this down, [*He
   writes.*]
That one may smile, and smile, and be a villain.
At least I'm sure it is true in Denmark.
[*Writing*] So, uncle, there you are. Now for my
   new motto.
It is "Adieu, adieu! Remember me."
I have sworn **vengeance**.[13]

Horatio. [*Offstage*] My lord, my lord—

Marcellus. [*Offstage*] Lord Hamlet.

Horatio. [*Offstage*] Heaven help him!

Hamlet. [*Aside*] So be it!

Horatio. [*Offstage*] Illo, ho, ho,[14] my lord!

Hamlet. Illo, ho, ho, boy! Come, bird, come!

[*Enter* Horatio *and* Marcellus.]

---

[11] Hamlet's mother, Gertrude.

[12] **villain**—evil person. Hamlet is referring to his uncle, King Claudius.

[13] **vengeance**—to get revenge, to punish King Claudius for murdering his father.

[14] Illo, ho, ho—the way that a falcon trainer would call those large hunting birds. Hamlet answers the same way.

Marcellus. How are you, my noble lord?

Horatio. What news, my lord?

Hamlet. [*To himself*] O, wonderful!

Horatio. Good my lord, tell us.

Hamlet. No. You'll tell other people.

Horatio. Not I, my lord, by heaven.

Marcellus. Nor I, my lord.

Hamlet. Who would think it? But you'll keep this secret?

Horatio and **Marcellus.** Yes, by heaven, my lord.

Hamlet. There isn't a villain living in Denmark that isn't a complete rascal.

Horatio. My lord, we don't need a ghost to come from the grave to tell us this.

Hamlet. Why, that's right. You are right. So, without more explaining, I think we should shake hands and part. You, go where your business and desire shall take you (for every man has business and desire, whatever it is). For my own poor part, I think I'll go and pray.

Horatio. These are but wild and confusing words, my lord.

Hamlet. I'm very sorry they upset you. Yes, very sorry.

Horatio. We're not upset, my lord.

Hamlet. Yes, by Saint Patrick,[15] there is much to upset you about what we have seen here, Horatio. It is a real ghost. I can tell you that. For your desire to know what it said, forget it. And now, good friends, as you are friends, scholars, and soldiers, let me ask you one small favor.

Horatio. What is it, my lord? We will do it.

Hamlet. Never tell anyone what you have seen tonight.

Horatio and **Marcellus.** My lord, we will not.

Hamlet. That's not enough. Swear it.

Horatio. In faith, my lord, I won't tell anyone.

Marcellus. Nor I, my lord, in faith.

Hamlet. Swear upon my sword.[16]

Marcellus. We have sworn, my lord, already.

Hamlet. Indeed, upon my sword, swear.

---

[15] St. Patrick, the patron saint of Ireland, supposedly had a special understanding of the place where souls go to be punished for their earthly sins before they can go to heaven.

[16] The handle of a sword made a cross, so they are swearing by their Christian religion.

Ghost. [*Beneath the stage*] Swear.

Hamlet. [*To the* Ghost] Ah, ha, boy! Do you speak? Are you there, honest fellow? [*To* Marcellus *and* Horatio] Come on—you hear this fellow—Say you will swear.

Horatio. Tell us what to swear, my lord.

Hamlet. Never to speak about what you have seen. Swear by my sword.

Ghost. [*Beneath*] Swear.

Hamlet. Come here, gentlemen, and lay your hands again upon my sword. Swear never to speak of what you have heard. Swear by my sword.

Ghost. [*Beneath*] Swear by his sword.

Hamlet. Once more, swear, good friends.

Horatio. O day and night, but this is very strange!

Hamlet. And therefore welcome it as you would welcome a stranger.
   There are more things in heaven and earth, Horatio,

Than are dreamt of in your **philosophy**.[17]
  But come.

Swear again, so help you, that no matter how
  strange or oddly I act,
(As I might in the future think it right to act
  strangely),[18]
That you, at such times seeing me, never shall
Fold your arms and shake your head,
Or say anything like, "We know what he's
  doing,"
Or "We could explain his actions, if we
  wanted to,"
Or "We could speak if we hadn't promised."
Or anything that might make someone think
You know something about what I am doing.
Never do that. So God help you on the day
  of judgment.

Ghost. [*Beneath the stage*] Swear.
Hamlet. [*To the* Ghost] Rest, rest, uneasy spirit!
  [Horatio *and* Marcellus *swear.*] So, gentlemen,
  With all my love I thank you.
  And I shall do what so poor a man as Hamlet
    may do

---

[17] **philosophy**—understanding of the world.
[18] Hamlet suggests that he may have to appear crazy later on.

To show his love and friendship to you, if God
    will let me.
Let us go in together, and keep quiet, I beg you.
The time is out of joint.[19] O cursed spite of fate
That ever I was born to set it right! Come, let's
    go together.

[*They all exit.*]

---

[19] The time is out of joint—everything is confused and wrong.

act two

In a room in Polonius's house, Polonius sends his servant Reynaldo to spy on Laertes at school in France. Ophelia tells Polonius that Hamlet seems to have gone mad. Polonius decides that Hamlet has gone mad because he loves Ophelia, and she refuses to see him. Polonius takes Ophelia to see Claudius.

[*Enter* Polonius *and* Reynaldo.]

Polonius. Give him this money and these notes, Reynaldo.

Reynaldo. I will, my lord.

Polonius. You shall do a very good job, good Reynaldo, if, before you visit him, you ask about his behavior.

Reynaldo. My lord, I planned on it.

Polonius. Marry, well said. Very well said. Listen, sir, first ask what other Danes are in Paris, and who, and how much money they have, and where they live. Ask who their friends are, and how much they spend. You will find by this indirect questioning if they know my son.[1] You will come closer to having your questions answered than if you ask them straight out. Pretend you know him a little. Say something like, "I know his father and his friends, and I've met him." Do you understand this, Reynaldo?

Reynaldo. Yes, very well, my lord.

Polonius. And you may say, "I know him; but, not well. But, if it's the man I'm thinking of, he's very wild, addicted to such and such." Then accuse him of whatever bad actions you wish to make up about him. Marry, none so bad as may **dishonor**[2] him. Pay attention to that. But, sir, say some immoral, wild, and usual faults that most often go along with young men who have some freedom.

Reynaldo. Such as gambling, my lord.

---

[1] Polonius is hiring Reynaldo to spy on Laertes.
[2] **dishonor**—disgrace; shame.

Polonius. Yes, or drinking, **fencing**,[3] swearing, quarrelling. You may go so far.

Reynaldo. My lord, that would dishonor him.

Polonius. Faith, no. Talk about his faults so carefully that they seem to be the results of youth and too much freedom.

Reynaldo. But, my good lord—

Polonius. Why should you do this?

Reynaldo. Yes, my lord. Why should I say these things about him?

Polonius. Marry, sir, here's my plan. I believe it is a clever trick.[4] If you say my son does these little bad actions, the person you're talking to, the person you would question about my son, if he has seen my son do these things, he will agree with you in this way. "Good sir," or "friend," or "gentleman," he will say according to where he came from or his education.

Reynaldo. Very good, my lord.

---

[3] **fencing**—sport fighting with swords.

[4] We are going to learn a lot about Polonius from these speeches. He talks too much, he interferes too much, and he likes to plot.

Polonius. And then, sir, he will say—he says—
what was I about to say? By the Mass,[5] I was
about to say something. Where did I stop?

Reynaldo. At "he will agree with you," at "friend"
and "gentleman."

Polonius. At "he will agree with you," yes, that's
it. He will agree with you this way: "I know the
gentleman. I saw him yesterday, or the other
day," (or then, with such and such a person).
"And, as you say, there he was gambling. There
he was drunk. There arguing at tennis," or perhaps, "I saw him enter a house of bad
reputation," or so forth. Do you see? Your bait of
small lies takes this fish of truth. And that is how
we men of wisdom and experience use indirect
ways to find the truth. You shall find out what
my son is doing by following my lecture and
advice. You understand me, don't you?

Reynaldo. My lord, I do.

Polonius. God be with you. Fare you well.

Reynaldo. Good my lord.

---

[5] Mass—church service. Polonius is swearing mildly.

Polonius. Watch what he does.

Reynaldo. I shall, my lord.

Polonius. And let him do his business.

Reynaldo. Yes, my lord.

Polonius. Farewell!
[*Exit* Reynaldo. *Enter* Ophelia, *very upset.*]
    Ophelia! What's the matter?

Ophelia. O, my lord, my lord. I have been so frightened!

Polonius. With what, in the name of God?

Ophelia. My lord, as I was sewing in my room, Lord Hamlet stood in front of me with his doublet[6] all unfastened. He had no hat upon his head, his stockings were dirty and hanging around his ankles, pale as his shirt, and his knees were knocking against each other. He had such a look as if he had been set free from hell to speak of horrors.

Polonius. Mad for your love?[7]

Ophelia. My lord, I do not know, but truly, I fear it.

---

[6] doublet—jacket.

[7] Polonius thinks Hamlet has been driven mad because Ophelia won't return his love.

Polonius. What did he say?

Ophelia. He took me by the wrist and held me hard.
　Then he held me away from him.
　And, with his other hand, like this, over his
　　forehead,
　He started to study my face
　As if he would draw it. He stared at me a
　　long time.
　At last, he shook my arm a little
　And nodded his head three times.
　He made so sad and deep a sigh that it seemed
　　to shatter
　And destroy him. When he finished, he let
　　me go,
　And, looking back at me,
　He seemed to find his way out of the room
　Without using his eyes. He went out without
　　looking,
　And, to the last, watched me.

Polonius. Come with me. I will find the king.
　This is the very madness of love,
　Whose violent nature destroys itself
　And leads the person to wild actions
　As often as any passion under heaven.
　I am sorry. Have you said anything to upset
　　him lately?

Ophelia. No, my good lord, but, as you commanded, I sent back his letters and did not let him visit me.

Polonius. That has made him mad. I am sorry that I did not pay closer attention to him before. I was afraid he was not serious about you and meant to ruin you. Curse my suspicious thoughts! By heaven, it is as normal to men of my age to have unreasonable suspicions as it is common for the younger sort to lack good sense. Come, let's go to the king. This must be known. If it is kept secret, it might cause more trouble than if we tell about his love.

[*They exit.*]

In a room in Elsinore castle, King Claudius asks Rosencrantz
and Guildenstern, Hamlet's boyhood friends, to find out
why Hamlet is behaving strangely. The ambassadors to
Norway report that the old Norwegian king has stopped
his nephew Fortinbras from trying to invade Denmark.
Polonius announces that Hamlet's madness was caused
by love. King Claudius agrees to join Polonius in spying
on Hamlet. When Hamlet meets Rosencrantz and
Guildenstern, he quickly realizes that they are spying for
King Claudius.

A group of traveling actors arrives. Hamlet asks them to
perform a play about a murder with some extra lines that
he has written. Alone again, Hamlet expresses shame that
he has shown less passion in revenging his father's murder
than an actor shows in a good speech.

[*Music plays. Enter* King Claudius, Queen Gertrude, Rosencrantz, Guildenstern, *and* Attendants.]

King Claudius. Welcome, dear Rosencrantz and Guildenstern! Much as we wanted to see you, we called you quickly because we need your help. You have probably heard something about Hamlet's sudden change. He does not look or act like he used to. I do not know what might have caused this, other than his father's death. I beg you both, since you were brought up with him and know him from your youth, to stay here in our court for a little time. Amuse him, and find out, as much as you can, if something troubles him that we don't know about. We might be able to help him if we can discover his problem.

Queen Gertrude. Good gentlemen, he has talked about you many times. I am sure there are not two men living that he likes better. We will give you whatever thanks a king can give if you will stay with us for a while, to help us.

Rosencrantz. Both your majesties might command us rather than ask us.

Guildenstern. But we both obey, and freely offer whatever we can do. Tell us what you want us to do.

King Claudius. Thanks, Rosencrantz and gentle Guildenstern.

Queen Gertrude. Thanks, Guildenstern and gentle Rosencrantz. I beg you to visit my too-much-changed son right away. Go, some of you, and take these gentlemen to Hamlet.

Guildenstern. Heaven make our presence and our actions pleasant and helpful to him!

Queen Gertrude. Yes, amen!

[*Exit* Rosencrantz, Guildenstern, *and some* Attendants. *Enter* Polonius.]

Polonius. The ambassadors from Norway, my good lord, are joyfully returned.

King Claudius. You are the father of good news.

Polonius. Am I, my lord? My duty is to do whatever I can for my God and my king. And I think, or else this brain of mine is not as quick as it used to be, that I have found the very cause of Hamlet's madness.

King Claudius. Tell us. I long to hear that.

Polonius. First see the ambassadors. My news shall be the dessert to that great feast.

King Claudius. Greet them and bring them in yourself. [*Exit* Polonius.] He tells me, my dear Gertrude, that he has found the source of all your son's strange actions.

Queen Gertrude. I am sure it is nothing but the main problem: his father's death and our too-quick marriage.

King Claudius. Well, we shall listen to him. [*Enter* Polonius, *with* Voltemand *and* Cornelius.] Welcome, my good friends! Say, Voltemand, what news comes from our brother, the King of Norway?

Voltemand. He sends his greetings. As soon as we mentioned the business, he stopped his nephew Fortinbras from raising an army. The king thought that his nephew was preparing to fight the king of Poland. But when he looked into it more closely, he found it was to fight against your highness. The king of Norway was sad and angry that he had been deceived because he was sick and old. He ordered Fortinbras to stop, which he did. Finally, Fortinbras promised his uncle never again to attack your majesty. The old king of Norway was so overcome with joy that he gave Fortinbras sixty thousand crowns[1] every year, and he ordered Fortinbras to use his soldiers against Poland. The king asks in this paper [*Giving* Claudius *a paper*] that you might give Fortinbras safe passage through our country to go to fight the Poles.

King Claudius. This pleases us. We will answer after we have read and thought about this. Meantime, we thank you for your good work. Go to your rest. Tonight we'll feast together. Welcome home!

[Voltemand *and* Cornelius *exit.*]

Polonius. This business is well ended. My lord, and madam, to argue about what majesty should be, what duty is, why day is day, night is night, and time is time, were nothing but to waste night, day, and time. Therefore, since brevity is the soul of wit,[2] and **tediousness**[3] the limbs and outward ornaments, I will be brief. Your noble son

---

[1] crowns—units of money in Norway.

[2] brevity is the soul of wit—saying much in a few words is the most important part of being clever. Shakespeare is making a joke. Polonius is not brief. Polonius uses big words to impress people.

[3] **tediousness**—boredom.

is mad. "Mad" I call it. For, to define true madness, what is it but to be nothing else but mad? But forget about that.

Queen Gertrude. More meaning, with less art.[4]

Polonius. Madam, I swear I use no art at all.
That he is mad, it is true. It is true that it is a pity,
And a pity it is that it is true. This word "it" is
    a foolish figure.[5]
But farewell "it," for my language is normal.
Let's agree that he was mad, then, and still
    is mad.
Let us find out the cause of this effect,
Or, rather say, the cause of this defect,
For this effect is caused by something defective.[6]
Thus it remains, and the remainder thus.
Take note of this.
I have a daughter (have while she is mine)
Who, in her duty and obedience, pay attention,
Has given me this letter. Now listen, and think.
[*Reads the letter from* Hamlet *to* Ophelia]
"To the heavenly and my soul's idol, the most
    beautified Ophelia,"—
That's a bad phrase, a horrible phrase.

---

[4] art—skill, as in making a speech. She is asking him to speak plainly.

[5] Polonius is talking about a figure of speech—language that means something different from the words used.

[6] Polonius's speeches show what is funny (or sad) about him.

"Beautified" is a bad phrase, but you shall
  hear. Thus:
[*Reads*] *"Keep this letter in your excellent white*
  bosom, etcetera."

Queen Gertrude. Did this come from Hamlet
to her?

Polonius. Good madam, wait a moment. I will tell
you.
[*Reads*] *"Doubt that the stars are fire.*
  Doubt that the sun does move.
Doubt truth to be a liar.
  But never doubt I love.
O dear Ophelia, I am not good at poetry. I do not
have the skill to tell you my pain. But believe that I
love you best, O most best. Adieu.
Yours forever, most dear lady, while this body is
mine, Hamlet."

This, my daughter has obediently shown me.
And she has given to me more of his messages,
including the time, ways, and places they were
to meet.

King Claudius. But how has she treated his love?

Polonius. What do you think of me?

King Claudius. You are a faithful and honorable man.

Polonius. I would like to prove so. But what might you think,
When I had seen this hot love on the wing
(As I guessed it, I must tell you, before my daughter told me).
What might you,
Or my dear majesty your queen here, think,
If I had helped this love grow, or paid no attention to it.
What might you think? No, I went to work.
I spoke to my daughter this way: "Lord Hamlet is a prince, out of your reach.
This must not be." Then I gave her instructions
That she should stay away from him,
Not see his notes, not receive his gifts.
She took my advice. He, not being allowed to see her (a short story to tell),
Fell into a sadness, then into a loss of hunger,
Then to sleeplessness, then into a weakness,
Then to a light-headedness. By these steps,
he moved into the madness where he now raves,
And we all mourn for him.

King Claudius. [*To* Gertrude] Do you think this is so?

Queen Gertrude. It may be, very likely.

Polonius. Has there been any time (I'd like to know) that I have said "This is so," when it proved not to be true?

King Claudius. Not that I know.

Polonius. [*Pointing first to his head and then to his shoulder*] Take *this* from *this,* if this be otherwise. If there are any clues, I will find where truth is hidden, even if it were hidden in the center of the Earth.

King Claudius. How can we find if this is true?

Polonius. You know, sometimes he walks for four hours here in the great hall.

Queen Gertrude. So he does, indeed.

Polonius. At such a time I'll let my daughter come to him. [*To the* King] You and I will hide behind an arras.[7] We will watch what happens. If he doesn't love her and has not been driven mad by her, send me away from you. Don't let me help you in the government anymore. Make me keep a farm.

---

[7] arras—hanging screen of rich tapestry fabric.

King Claudius. We will try it.

[*Enter* Hamlet, *reading a book.*]

Queen Gertrude. But, look, where the poor wretch[8] comes reading.

Polonius. Leave, I beg both of you. I'll talk to him now.

[*Exit* King Claudius, Queen Gertrude, *and* Attendants.]

O, excuse me. How is my good Lord Hamlet?

Hamlet. Well, God-a-mercy.[9]

Polonius. Do you know me, my lord?

Hamlet. Very well. You are a fishmonger.[10]

Polonius. Not I, my lord.

Hamlet. Then I wish you were so honest a man.

Polonius. Honest, my lord!

Hamlet. Yes, sir. To be honest, in this world, is to be one man out of ten thousand.

Polonius. That's very true, my lord.

---

[8] wretch—miserable, unhappy person.

[9] God-a-mercy—God have mercy on you. This greeting was used often for someone socially beneath the speaker.

[10] Hamlet pretends to be mad. He says that Polonius is a fishmonger, a fish seller (also slang for a procurer of prostitutes). It could mean that "something's fishy" or that "Polonius smells bad."

Hamlet. [*Reading*] "For if the sun causes maggots[11] in a dead dog, being good flesh for kissing"[12]— Have you a daughter?

Polonius. I have, my lord.

Hamlet. Don't let her walk in the sun. Conception[13] is a blessing, but not as your daughter may conceive. Friend, be careful of her.

Polonius. [*Aside*] What do you think of that? Still talking about my daughter. Yet he didn't know me at first. He said I was a fishmonger. He is far gone. And truly, in my youth I suffered much for love, almost as much as this. I'll speak to him again. [*To* Hamlet] What do you read, my lord?

Hamlet. Words, words, words.

Polonius. What is the matter,[14] my lord?

Hamlet. With who?

Polonius. I mean, the matter that you read, my lord.

Hamlet. Lies, sir. For this joker says here that old men have gray beards, that their faces are wrinkled, their eyes ooze sticky stuff, that they lack

---

[11] maggots—fly larva. These worms eat decaying things.

[12] When the sun shines on something, it is said to be kissing it.

[13] conception—*Wordplay:* understanding or getting pregnant.

[14] matter—*Wordplay:* Polonius means "subject matter," but Hamlet pretends to understand it as "quarrel."

cleverness, and they have very weak legs. All of which, sir, I most powerfully and strongly believe. But I don't think it is polite to have it written down. For you, sir, would be as old as I am, if like a crab you could go backward.[15]

Polonius. [*Aside*] Though this is madness, yet there is method[16] in it. [*To* Hamlet] Will you walk out of the air, my lord?

Hamlet. Into my grave?

Polonius. Indeed, that is out of the air.[17] [*Aside*] Sometimes his replies are very meaningful! Sometimes there is truth in madness that reason and sanity can't give. I will leave him and quickly find a way for a meeting between him and my daughter.— [*To* Hamlet] My honorable lord, I will take my leave of you.

Hamlet. You cannot, sir, take from me any thing that I will more willingly part with—except my life, except my life, except my life.

Polonius. Fare well, my lord.

Hamlet. [*Aside*] These boring old fools!

---

[15] Hamlet says that Polonius would be as old as Hamlet if Polonius could go back in time.

[16] method—sense.

[17] Polonius wants Hamlet to get out of the cold air. Hamlet gives the words another meaning. He would, indeed, be out of the air if he were in his grave.

[*Enter* Rosencrantz *and* Guildenstern.]

Polonius. If you are trying to find the Lord Hamlet, there he is.

Rosencrantz. [*To* Polonius] God save you, sir!

[Polonius *exits.*]

Guildenstern. My honored lord!

Rosencrantz. My most dear lord!

Hamlet. My excellent good friends! How are you, Guildenstern? Ah, Rosencrantz! Good lads, how are you both?

Rosencrantz. Like most people.

Guildenstern. Happy, but we are not too happy. On Fortune's cap we are not at the very top.

Hamlet. Nor the soles of her shoe?

Rosencrantz. Neither, my Lord.

Hamlet. What's the news?

Rosencrantz. None, my Lord, but that the world's grown honest.

Hamlet. Then the end of the world must be near. But your news is not true. Let me question you carefully. What have you, my good friends, done to Fortune that she sends you to prison here?

Guildenstern. Prison, my lord?

Hamlet. Denmark's a prison.

Rosencrantz. Then the world is one.

Hamlet. A very big one in which there are many cells and dungeons. Denmark is one of the worst.

Rosencrantz. We don't think so, my lord.

Hamlet. Why, then, it is not one to you. Nothing is either good or bad unless thinking makes it so. To me, it is a prison.

Rosencrantz. Why then, your **ambition**[18] makes it one. It is too small for your mind.

Hamlet. O God, I could be locked in a nutshell and count myself the king of infinite space, if I didn't have bad dreams.

Guildenstern. Your dreams are, indeed, ambition, for ambition is made out of dreams.

Hamlet. A dream itself is just a shadow.

Rosencrantz. Truly, and I believe ambition to be so unimportant that it is just a shadow of a shadow.

---

[18] **ambition**—strong desire for power or success.

Hamlet. Then our beggars have bodies, and our monarchs and heroes are the beggars' shadows.[19] Shall we go to the court? For, by my faith, I cannot continue with this kind of talk.

Rosencrantz and **Guildenstern.** We'll wait on you.

Hamlet. No you will not be my servants, for, to speak to you like an honest man, I am most poorly waited on.[20] But, as friends, why are you at Elsinore?

Rosencrantz. To visit you, my lord. No other reason.

Hamlet. Beggar that I am, I am even poor in thanks. But I thank you, and I am sure, dear friends, my thanks are not enough for your effort. Did someone send for you? Did you come here on your own? Come, come, tell me the truth. Speak up.

Guildenstern. What should we say, my lord?

Hamlet. [Hamlet *sees that they are uncomfortable.*] Anything but what is true. You were sent for. I can tell by the guilty looks that you are not able to hide. I know the good king and queen have sent for you.

---

[19] Since beggars have no ambition, they are the only humans with solid bodies. Kings and heroes, who are ruled by ambition, are only the beggars' shadows.

[20] *Wordplay:* They mean they will go with him, but Hamlet uses *waited* to mean a waiter or servant who brings food.

Rosencrantz. Why would they, my lord?

Hamlet. That, you must tell me. Let me ask you seriously, by our friendship, by the happy times in our youth, by whatever you can think of for an oath, tell me truthfully, were you sent for?

Rosencrantz. [*Aside to* Guildenstern] What should I say?

Hamlet. I am waiting. If you are my friends, tell me.

Guildenstern. My lord, we were sent for.

Hamlet. I will tell you why. Then you won't have to tell the king and queen that you told me. I have recently lost all my happiness. I don't know why. I do not exercise. I am so depressed that this great Earth seems dead. The air and the sky—this majestic roof decorated with golden light—seem to me evil-smelling and sick. What a piece of work is a man. He is noble in reason, infinite in abilities, well-framed and admirable in form and movement. In action he is like an angel. In understanding he is like a god. Man is the beauty of the world, the perfect animal— and yet, to me, what is this perfection of dust?

I am not delighted by man—nor by woman either, though your smiles seem to say so.[21]

Rosencrantz. My lord, I wasn't thinking that.

Hamlet. Why did you laugh then, when I said I was not delighted by man?

Rosencrantz. I was thinking, my lord, that if man cannot delight you, then you won't want to see the actors who are coming to entertain you. We passed them on the way here.

Hamlet. The actor who plays the part of the king will be welcome—his majesty shall receive his praise. The actor who plays the hero shall show his skill with the sword. The lover shall not sigh for nothing. The bad tempered character will end his part in peace. The clown shall make those laugh who are ready to laugh. The lady[22] shall say her mind. What players are they?

Rosencrantz. The ones you enjoyed so much in the city.

Hamlet. Why are they traveling? If they stayed in the city, both their good name and their profits would grow.

---

[21] Through the rest of the play, Hamlet tries to find out what has made him so depressed and unreasonable. This mystery is at the heart of the play.

[22] The lady—the actor playing the female role.

Rosencrantz. There is a new fad. Child actors are getting all the parts.

[*Trumpets sound as the actors enter.*]

Guildenstern. Here are the players.

Hamlet. [*To* Rosencrantz *and* Guildenstern] Gentlemen, you are welcome to Elsinore. Shake hands with me, so I may welcome you as warmly as I will welcome these players. You are welcome. But my uncle-father and aunt-mother are deceived.

Guildenstern. In what way, my dear lord?

Hamlet. I am only mad when the wind is blowing from the north-north-west. When the wind is from the south, I know a hawk from a handsaw.[23]

[Polonius *enters.*]

Polonius. Welcome, gentlemen.

Hamlet. Listen Guildenstern, and you too, both of you. That great baby there is not yet out of his diaper.

---

[23] Hamlet says he is only crazy at certain times. At other times he can tell one thing from another.

Rosencrantz. Perhaps this is his second time in diapers. They say an old man has a second childhood.

Hamlet. I will predict that he comes to tell me about the players. Listen. [*Hamlet pretends he is in the middle of a conversation.*] That's right, sir, a Monday morning.

Polonius. My lord, I have news to tell you.

Hamlet. My lord, I have news to tell you. When Roscius[24] was an actor in Rome. . . .

Polonius. The actors have come here, my lord.

Hamlet. Buzz, buzz. Old news.

Polonius. On my honor—

Hamlet. Then each actor came on his ass.[25]

Polonius. They are the best actors in the world, either for tragedy, comedy, history, pastoral, pastoral-comical, historical-pastoral, tragical-historical, tragical-comical-historical-pastoral, individual scenes, or epic poems. Tragedy cannot be too tragic or comedy too comic for them. For

---

[24] Roscius was a famous actor in ancient Roman times.

[25] Hamlet is quoting an old song.

following a script or for **improvising**²⁶—these
are the only men.

[*Enter the* Players.]

Hamlet. [*To the* Players] You are all welcome. I am
glad to see you well. Welcome, good friends. My
old friend, you have grown a beard since I saw
you last. What, my young lady, you are nearer to
heaven than when I saw you last.²⁷ Pray God
your voice hasn't broken. Masters, you are all
welcome. Give us a speech right away. We cannot
wait. Come, a passionate speech.

First Player. What speech, my lord?

Hamlet. I once heard you give a speech from a
play that was never acted. The common people
would not have liked it, but it was an excellent
play. There were no dirty jokes or showing off.
It came from natural skill and was wholesome
and sweet. It was the story of the fall of ancient
Troy. If you can remember it, start at this line—
let me see—
The rugged Pyrrhus,²⁸ he whose black arms,
Black as his purpose, seemed like the night,

---

²⁶ **improvising**—making up as one goes along.

²⁷ The boy actor who plays the young lady has grown older and taller, nearer
to his death and nearer to going to heaven.

²⁸ Hamlet is remembering another play about a hero, Pyrrhus, who revenged
the death of his father by killing an old king, Priam.

Now is covered with red blood—
With blood of fathers, mothers, daughters, sons
Baked on him by the heat of the day.
This lends an unholy light to the murder of the king.
Roasted in wrath[29] and fire, the hellish Pyrrhus goes
after old grandfather Priam.

Go on, start there.

Polonius. Before God, my lord, well spoken, with good accent.

First Player. *Soon he finds him fighting the Greeks.*
Unequally matched, Pyrrhus drives at the old king
in rage.
His sword above the milk-white head of the old king
Seemed to stick in the air.
But now new anger sets him to work again.
And with no remorse, his sword
Now falls on the king.
The senseless city seemed to feel the blow.
Out, out, you loose woman, Fortune! All you gods
Take away her power—

Polonius. This is too long.

Hamlet. It will go to the barber with your beard. Please, go on. [*Aside*] He wants a dance or a

---

[29] *wrath*—fierce anger.

dirty story, or he falls asleep. [*To the* Players] Go
on. Come to Hecuba.[30]

First Player. *But who has seen the wailing queen*
Run barefoot up and down, drowning the flames
With her blinding tears, a rag around her head
Instead of a queenly crown?
Whoever saw this would have shouted bitter words
* 'gainst fortune.*
If the gods themselves had seen her then
When the sword cut off her husband's limbs
Her wailing would have made the tears of heaven fall.

Polonius. Look, the player is pale and crying! [*To
the* First Player] I beg you stop.

Hamlet. Enough. I'll hear the rest soon. [*To
Polonius*] My lord, will you see the players well
taken care of? They give us the summary and
history of our time.

Polonius. My lord, I will give them what they
deserve.

Hamlet. By God's body, man, give them much
better. If every man got what he deserves, we
would all be whipped. Treat them as you would

---

[30] Hecuba, the Queen of Troy, is the old king's wife. She represents
suffering. She had to watch her city being destroyed and her husband
and children killed.

treat yourself. The less they deserve, the more goodness you deserve for your kindness. Take them in.

Polonius. Come, sirs.

Hamlet. Follow him, friends. We'll hear a play tomorrow. [*To the* First Player] Listen, old friend, can you play *The Murder of Gonzago?*

First Player. Yes, my lord.

Hamlet. Perform it tomorrow night. Could you memorize a speech of about a dozen lines which I will write and put in the play?

First Player. Yes, my lord.

Hamlet. Very well. [*To all the* Players] Follow that lord, and don't make fun of him.

[*Exit* Polonius *and the* Players.]

[*To* Rosencrantz *and* Guildenstern] My good friends, I'll leave you until tonight. You are welcome to Elsinore.

Rosencrantz. Good day, my lord.

Hamlet. Yes, so goodbye to you. [*Exit* Rosencrantz *and* Guildenstern.] Now I am alone.

O what a rogue and peasant slave[31] am I!
Is it not monstrous that this player here,
In a play, in a dream of sadness,
Could force himself to believe so much
That he cried in sorrow. His voice broke in a sob.
And all for nothing!
For Hecuba!
What's Hecuba to him, or he to Hecuba
That he should weep for her? What would he do
If he had the real reasons for sorrow that I have?
He would drown the stage with tears and split
    the ear with horrid speech.
He would make the guilty go mad, and
    frighten the innocent,
Confuse the ignorant, and amaze our eyes
    and ears.
Yet I, a dull-spirited creature, **mope**[32] around
Like a dreamer not able to do anything,
Or say anything—no, not for a king, who was
    murdered.
Am I a coward?
Who calls me villain? Hits me across the head?
Pulls on my beard? Twists my nose?

---

[31] peasant slave—low-class person.
[32] **mope**—brood; sulk.

Calls me a liar and makes me take the insults?
Who does this to me? Ha! By God's wounds!
I should take it.
I am a coward.
I should have filled all the region's **vultures**[33]
With this slave's[34] guts. Bloody, immoral villain!
Pitiless, treacherous, evil, unnatural villain!
O vengeance!
Why, what an ass I am! This is most fine.
That I, the son of a dear father who was
    murdered,
Told by heaven and hell to seek revenge,
Can only start to curse like a whore or a
    kitchen servant!
Fie on it! Think, my brains!—Hum, I have heard
That a guilty man watching a play
Has sometimes been led to admit his guilt.
For murder will speak some way, though it has
    no tongue.
I'll have these players
Play something like the murder of my father
For my uncle to see. I'll watch him carefully.
If he turns pale, I'll know what I must do.

---

[33] **vultures**—birds that eat dead meat.
[34] this slave's—King Claudius's.

The ghost I have seen may be a devil. The
    devil has the power
To take on a pleasing shape. Yes, and perhaps
He uses my weakness and sorrow
To deceive me and lead me to hell.
I need more proof. The play's the thing
Wherein I'll catch the conscience of the king.

[Hamlet *exits.*]

act three

In a room in Elsinore castle, Rosencrantz and Guildenstern admit to the king that they can't find the cause of Hamlet's madness. Polonius arranges a meeting between Ophelia and Hamlet. Polonius and King Claudius secretly watch. When Ophelia tries to return his gifts, Hamlet suddenly turns on her and says he never loved her. After Hamlet leaves, Claudius decides that Hamlet's madness is not caused by love. He says he will send Hamlet on a mission to England. Polonius persuades the king to wait until the queen has a chance to talk to Hamlet.

[*Enter* King Claudius, Queen Gertrude, Polonius, Ophelia, Rosencrantz, Guildenstern, *and* Lords.]

King Claudius. And can't you find out why he acts in this **distracted**[1] way, like a mad man?

---

[1] **distracted**—unsettled; disturbed.

Rosencrantz. He confesses that he feels himself distracted. But he will not say what causes it.

Guildenstern. Nor do we find him eager to be questioned. He keeps away from us with a crafty madness when we try to question him.

Queen Gertrude. Did he welcome you?

Rosencrantz. Like a gentleman.

Guildenstern. But he didn't act naturally.

Queen Gertrude. Did you talk him into any entertainment?

Rosencrantz. Madam, we told him about the arrival of some players. He seemed happy to hear about them. They are here at the court, and, I think, they have already been ordered to play before him tonight.

Polonius. It is most true. And he begged me to ask your majesties to hear and see the play.

King Claudius. With all my heart, and I'm happy he is interested in them. Good gentlemen, try to keep him interested.

Rosencrantz. We shall, my Lord.

[Rosencrantz, Guildenstern, *and* Lords *exit.*]

King Claudius. Sweet Gertrude, leave us too, for we have secretly sent for Hamlet that he may meet Ophelia here as if by accident. Her father and I, lawful spies, will hide so that we will see but be unseen. We will judge by their meeting if it is love that makes him suffer.

Queen Gertrude. I shall obey you. And for your part, Ophelia, I hope that your beauty is the happy cause of Hamlet's wildness. So shall I hope your goodness will bring him to his senses again. This would be good for both of you.

Ophelia. Madam, I wish it may.

[Queen Gertrude *exits*.]

Polonius. Ophelia, walk here. Your majesty, so please you, we will hide ourselves. [*To* Ophelia] Read this prayer book. This will give you a reason for being here alone. We are often to blame for doing this sort of thing. We pretend to be good and holy to cover our tricks.

King Claudius. [*Aside*] O, it's too true! What he says stings my conscience! The whore's cheek is just as ugly under its makeup as my ugly deed is under my painted words.[2] O heavy burden!

---

[2] Claudius is admitting to having done an evil deed.

Polonius. I hear him coming. Let's hide, my lord.

[King Claudius *and* Polonius *exit.* Hamlet *enters.*]

Hamlet. To be or not to be—that is the question:[3]
Whether 'tis nobler in the mind to suffer
The slings and arrows of outrageous fortune,
Or to take arms against a sea of troubles
And, by opposing, end them. To die, to sleep—
No more—and by a sleep to say we end
The heartache and the thousand natural shocks
That life gives us. It is an ending
Devoutly[4] to be wished. To die, to sleep—
To sleep, perhaps to dream. Ay, there's the rub,[5]
For in that sleep of death, what dreams
    may come
When we have removed ourself from this life
Must make us stop and think.
That's why we put up with unhappiness for
    so long.
For who could stand the pains and humiliation
    of time,
The oppressor's wrong,[6] the proud man's insults,

---

[3] The first seven lines of this famous speech are in Shakespeare's words. Hamlet is asking whether he should continue living and put up with his troubles in life or fight against them and probably be destroyed. There is also the possibility that he is thinking about suicide.

[4] **Devoutly**—sincerely; earnestly.

[5] rub—problem.

[6] oppressor's wrong—evil done by a powerful person.

The pains of unreturned love, the law's slowness,

The rudeness of those in power,

When he himself might end it

With a bare bodkin?[7] Who would carry such

burdens,

Who would grunt and sweat under a hard life,

Except that the fear of something after death,

The undiscovered country from which

No traveler returns, weakens our actions?

It makes us bear those problems we have

Rather than run to others that we don't

know about

So our knowledge makes us all cowards.

Our natural courage is made weak by thought,

And important actions are not done—Wait

a minute!

The fair Ophelia! [*To* Ophelia] Nymph,[8]

remember to pray for my sins.

Ophelia. Good my lord, how have you been since
I saw you last?

Hamlet. I humbly thank you, well.

---

[7] bare bodkin—small knife or dagger. Hamlet says why put up with all this
when it could be settled with a dagger.

[8] Nymph—one of the minor goddesses of Greek mythology, a beautiful
young woman.

Ophelia. My lord, I have some gifts you gave me that I have long wished to return to you. I pray you, let me give them to you now.

Hamlet. No, not I. I never gave you anything.[9]

Ophelia. My honored lord, you know very well you did. And, with them, words that were so sweet that they made the gifts sweeter. Take these back, for to the noble mind, rich gifts become poor when givers prove unkind. [*She hands him a small package.*] There, my lord.

Hamlet. [*Laughs.*] Ha, ha! Are you honest?[10]

Ophelia. My lord?

Hamlet. Are you fair?[11]

Ophelia. What do you mean?

Hamlet. That if you are honest and fair, your modesty should not let anyone get close to your beauty.

Ophelia. Could beauty, my lord, have a better friend than honesty?

---

[9] Is this part of Hamlet's plan to appear to be mad? Perhaps he is saying that he has changed since he gave her presents.

[10] honest—*Wordplay:* are you telling the truth? Are you innocent? Are you modest?

[11] fair—*Wordplay:* beautiful, but it also means "doing the right thing."

Hamlet. Yes, truly, for the power of beauty will sooner change honesty to sin than the power of honesty can change beauty into goodness. I used to think this was not true, but now I see the proof. I loved you once.

Ophelia. Indeed, my lord, you made me believe you did.

Hamlet. You should not have believed me, for our goodness cannot cover our sinful nature. I never loved you.

Ophelia. I was more sadly deceived.

Hamlet. Get thee to a nunnery.[12] Do you want to be the mother of sinners? I am reasonably good, but I could accuse myself of such things that it would have been better if my mother had not given birth to me. I am very proud, revengeful, and ambitious. I can call up more evil deeds than I have thoughts to put them in, imagination to give them shape, or time to act them in. What should fellows like me do, crawling between Earth and heaven? All men are evil, all. Believe none of us. Go to a nunnery. Where's your father?

---

[12] nunnery—convent, a building where nuns live. In crude humor, the word was also used to mean "brothel."

Ophelia. At home, my lord.

Hamlet. Lock him in so he cannot be a fool anywhere except in his own house. Farewell.

Ophelia. O, help him, you sweet heavens!

Hamlet. If you marry, I'll give you this curse for your wedding gift. Even if you are as cold as ice, as pure as snow, you shall not escape lying gossip. Go to a nunnery. Farewell. Or, if you must marry, marry a fool. For wise men know well that wives are not faithful. To a nunnery, go, and quickly too. Farewell.

Ophelia. Heavenly powers, help him!

Hamlet. I know very well how you paint your face[13] too. God has given you one face, and you women make yourselves another. You show yourselves off. You tease men when you walk and talk. You pretend to be innocent. Go to, I'll have nothing more to do with it. It has made me mad. I say, we will have no more marriage. Those that are married already, all but one, shall live.[14] The rest shall stay as they are. To a nunnery, go.

---

[13] paint your face—wear makeup or appear to be what you are not. Ophelia, in fact, is acting as a spy for her father.

[14] This is a threat on King Claudius's life. The king hears this from his hiding spot and probably understands the threat.

[Hamlet *exits.*]

Ophelia. O, what a noble mind has been ruined! He was the perfect gentleman, soldier, scholar, the hope of Denmark. He was the mirror of proper behavior, the model for men. The most respected of men, quite, quite ruined! And I am the most sad and miserable of women. I was given the honey of his loving promises.—I now see that noble and intelligent mind, like sweet bells jangled, out of time and harsh. That perfect youth is ruined by madness. O, woe is me, to have seen what I have seen, and now to see what I see!

[*Enter* King Claudius *and* Polonius.]

King Claudius. Love! He's not thinking about love. Nor was what he said madness, though it was a little confused. There's something in his soul on which his sadness sits, like a bird on its eggs. I fear he will hatch it, and it will be dangerous. To prevent this danger, I have decided to send him quickly to England to demand the money England owes us.[15] Perhaps the change of scenery and climate will help him forget

---

[15] For a while England paid Denmark money to keep from being attacked— protection money.

whatever is bothering him. What do you think of this plan?

Polonius. It's a good idea, but I still believe the loss of love started his sadness. How now, Ophelia! You need not tell us what Lord Hamlet said. We heard it all. My lord, do as you please. But, if you agree, after the play, let his queen-mother privately ask him to tell about his sadness. Let her speak plainly with him. I'll be where I can hear them, if you agree. If she cannot get him to say what the trouble is, then send him to England, or lock him up where you wisely think best.

King Claudius. It shall be so. Madness in great ones must be watched.

[*They exit.*]

*In a hall in Elsinore castle, Hamlet instructs the actors.
Then he asks Horatio to help him watch King Claudius's
reactions to the play. The actors perform the play. Its story
is very like the murder of Hamlet's father, as told by the
ghost. When the actors are showing the murder, King
Claudius rushes out of the room. Hamlet tells Horatio that
this proves that the ghost is telling the truth. Rosencrantz
and Guildenstern tell Hamlet that King Claudius is very
angry and that Queen Gertrude wants to speak to him
privately. Hamlet promises himself that he will punish his
mother only with words, not actions.*

[*Enter* Hamlet *and* Players.]

Hamlet. [*Speaking to the* Players[1]] Speak the speech,
I beg you, as I told it to you, gently. But if you
say it without knowing what it means, as many

---

[1] Of course, this is also Shakespeare talking to actors. Here he lets us see him
in his director role.

players do, I would rather have the town crier[2] speak my lines. Don't toss your arms around wildly like this, but be gentle. For in the very flood, storm, and whirlwind of your feelings, you must learn and use control. Then you can deliver your speeches smoothly. O, it upsets me to the soul to hear a loud, overdressed actor shout his feelings, to split the ears of the groundlings,[3] who for the most part can't enjoy anything but simple shows and noise. I would have such a fellow whipped for his noise. It out-Herods Herod.[4] I beg you, don't do it.

First Player. I promise your honor.

Hamlet. Be not too tame either, but let your own common sense teach you. Fit the action to the word, the word to the action, but do not do anything on stage that you wouldn't see a real person do. For anything overdone ruins the reason for acting. The goal of acting, from the earliest plays until now, was and is to hold a mirror up to life, to show goodness her own

---

[2] town crier—man who made public announcements by shouting them on the streets.

[3] groundlings—people who paid the least to see the play and stood on the ground in front of the stage.

[4] Herod, from the Bible, was a favorite, loud character in popular plays.

face, evil her own appearance, and to show us what we really look like now and why we act the way we do. If this is overdone, or done badly, it makes the fools laugh. But it makes the wise feel sad. For you, the judgment of one who knows must be more important than a whole theater of others. O, there are players that I have seen play and heard others praise highly who don't talk or walk like real people. They strutted and shouted so much that I thought some of nature's workmen had made them, and not made them well—they imitated people so badly.

First Player. I hope we have not done that too much, sir.

Hamlet. O, don't do it at all. And don't let the actors who play your clowns say any more than is written for them. Some of them will laugh at their own jokes, and so some of the audience will laugh too. In the meantime, some important point of the play can't be heard. That's wicked, and shows a most pitiful ambition in the fool that does it. Go and get ready.

[Players *exit. Enter* Polonius, Rosencrantz, *and* Guildenstern.]

How now, my lord! Will the king hear the play?

Polonius. And the queen too, and as soon as possible.

Hamlet. Tell the players to hurry. [Polonius *exits*.]
Will you two help them to get ready?

Rosencrantz. We will, my lord.

[Rosencrantz *and* Guildenstern *exit*.]

Hamlet. Where are you, Horatio!

[*Enter* Horatio.]

Horatio. Here, sweet lord, at your service.

Hamlet. Horatio, you are as good a man as I have
ever spoken to.

Horatio. O, my dear lord—

Hamlet. No, do not think I say this to flatter you,
For what can I hope to get from you?
You have less money than good spirits.
Ever since I could judge men, my soul has
chosen you as its friend.
For you have suffered everything and showed
nothing.
Give me a man who thanks Fortune for good
or bad luck.
Give me a man who is not passion's slave, and
I will wear him
In my heart's center, as I do you.

—But enough of this.—

There is a play tonight that the king will see.

One scene is very much like my father's death.

I beg you, carefully watch my uncle

When you see that scene. If his hidden guilt

Does not show itself when one speech[5] is said,

> then it is a false and evil ghost that we
> have seen.

> Watch him carefully. I will not take my eyes off
> his face,

And afterwards, we will compare what we
> have seen.

Horatio. Nothing he does will escape me.

[*Trumpets sound.*]

Hamlet. They are coming to the play. I must look like I am not doing anything. Find a seat.

[*Enter* Musicians *playing trumpets and drums. Enter* King Claudius, Queen Gertrude, Polonius, Ophelia, Rosencrantz, Guildenstern, Lords, *and* Attendants.]

King Claudius. How is our cousin Hamlet?

Hamlet. Excellent, in faith. I eat only air filled with promises.

---

[5] one speech—the speech Hamlet has written to add to the play.

King Claudius. I don't understand you, Hamlet. You didn't answer my question.

Hamlet. [*To himself*] They don't answer my questions either. [*To* Polonius] My lord, you acted once in a play at the university, you say?

Polonius. I did, my lord, and was thought to be a good actor.

Hamlet. What did you play?

Polonius. I acted the part of Julius Caesar.[6] I was killed in the Capitol. Brutus killed me.

Hamlet. It was a brute part of him to kill so capital a calf there.[7] Are the actors ready?

Rosencrantz. Yes, my lord. They are waiting until you are ready.

Queen Gertrude. Come here, my dear Hamlet. Sit by me.

Hamlet. No, good mother. Here's a more attractive magnet. [Hamlet *sits by* Ophelia.]

---

[6] Shakespeare also wrote a play about the death of Julius Caesar. Caesar was stabbed to death.

[7] *Wordplay:* this is a series of puns, playing on the double meaning of the words. *Brute,* meaning animal, suggests Brutus. Caesar was killed in the Capitol building. Hamlet says they sacrificed Caesar like they might sacrifice a calf. But, *calf* also meant a fool. So Hamlet is calling Polonius a fool.

Polonius. [*To* King Claudius] O, ho! Did you notice that?

Hamlet. Lady, shall I lie in your lap?[8]

[*Lying down at* Ophelia's *feet*]

Ophelia. No, my lord.

Hamlet. I mean, my head in your lap?

Ophelia. Yes, my lord.

Hamlet. What did you think I meant?

Ophelia. I think nothing, my lord. You are joking.

Hamlet. Who, me?

Ophelia. Yes, my lord.

Hamlet. O, God is the best comic of them all. What else can a man do but joke? For see how cheerful my mother looks, and my father died only two hours ago.[9]

Ophelia. No, it was twice two months ago, my Lord.

Hamlet. That long? I must get an expensive black suit to show my sorrow! O heavens! He died two months ago, and he's not forgotten yet?

---

[8] Shall I put myself in your power? A sexual interpretation is meant as well.

[9] For Hamlet, time has stopped since he saw the ghost two hours ago.

Then there's hope a great man may be remembered for at least six months. But, by Our Lady,[10] he must have churches built in his name, or else he will be forgotten.

[*Music plays. The actors enter to put on a dumb show or mime.[11] Enter a* King *and a* Queen *very lovingly. The* Queen *hugs him, and he hugs her. He lies down on a bed of flowers. She, seeing him asleep, leaves him. Soon, the poisoner enters, takes off the sleeping man's crown, kisses it, pours poison in the* King's *ears, and exits. The* Queen *returns, finds the* King *dead, and acts as if she is very upset. The* Poisoner, *with two or three others, comes in again, and seems to comfort her. The dead body is carried away. The* Poisoner *tries to attract the* Queen *with gifts. She seems to not be interested in him at first, but in the end she accepts his love. They exit.*]

Ophelia. What does this mean, my lord?

Hamlet. It means secret evil.

Ophelia. Perhaps this actor will tell us what the play will be about.

---

[10] Our Lady—Jesus's mother, Mary. Hamlet is swearing for emphasis.

[11] The dumb show was a pantomime or simple telling of the coming play, without words. It gave the basic story and made things easier for the audience to understand.

[*Enter the actor who will give the prologue, or introduction to the play.*]

Hamlet. He will tell us. These actors can't keep a secret.

Actor giving Prologue. We ask your mercy and your patience for us and for our tragedy.

[*He exits.*]

Hamlet. Is this a prologue or a few words cut inside a ring?

Ophelia. It is very brief, my Lord.

Hamlet. As brief as a woman's love.

[*Enter the* Player King *and* Player Queen.]

Player King. *We have long been united in sacred marriage.*

Player Queen. *And we will be married even longer. But woe is me. Lately you are so sick, so unhappy. I am afraid for you. But I am a woman and a woman who loves you. The littlest fear grows serious where love is great.*

Player King. *I am growing old and will soon die, leaving you behind. You will be honored and loved, and I hope that one who loves you as much as I do will marry. . . .*

Player Queen. *Never. I could never love another. No woman marries a second husband except those who killed the first.*

Hamlet. That's harsh.

Player King. *I do believe you think what you now speak. But people often change their minds. Our time in this world is short. When people die, they are quickly forgotten, and quickly we think in other ways. So you think you will never marry a second husband, but such thoughts will die with your first husband.*

Player Queen. *I will never marry another. I will be a* **hermit**[12] *before I marry anyone else. May I never have joy on earth or heaven if I ever marry anyone else.*

Hamlet. She should not break her promise now.

Player King. *You have promised me. Sweet, leave me for a while. I am very tired and need to rest.*

[*He sleeps.*]

Player Queen. *May sleep soothe your brain.*
And, may there never be any trouble between us twain.[13]

[*The* Player Queen *exits.*]

---

[12] **hermit**—person who lives away from everyone.

[13] *twain*—two.

Hamlet. [*To his mother*] Madam, do you like the play?

Queen Gertrude. The lady does protest too much, I think.[14]

Hamlet. O, but she will keep her word.

King Claudius. Do you know this play? Is there anything we would not like in it?[15]

Hamlet. No, no. They are just joking. They jokingly poison. There is nothing in it you wouldn't like.

King Claudius. What is the name of this play?

Hamlet. *The Mousetrap.* The name must mean something. This play is like a real murder that was done in Vienna. Gonzago is the duke's name, his wife is Baptista. You shall see it all. It's about an evil event, but what of that? Your majesty, because we are innocent, it's not about us. [*Enter the actor playing* Lucianus.] This is Lucianus, nephew to the King.

Ophelia. You are as good as a chorus, my lord.[16]

Hamlet. [*To the* Players] Begin the murder. Begin.

---

[14] The lady is not believable because she is making too much fuss.

[15] Claudius is not happy with the subject matter of the play. He wants to be reassured.

[16] The chorus in a play would explain things.

Lucianus. *My thoughts are evil. My hands are ready. I have the right drug and the time to use it. There is no one to see this murder. You evil, deadly poison, take away his life now.*

[*He pours the poison in the Player King's ear.*]

Hamlet. [Hamlet *is obviously very nervous and excited. He continues to explain the play.*] He poisoned the king in the garden. The king's name is Gonzago. This story is true. It's written in good Italian. You shall soon see how he steals the dead king's wife.

[King Claudius *stands up.*]

Ophelia. The king rises.

Hamlet. What, frightened by a play?

Queen Gertrude. Are you all right, my lord?

Polonius. Stop the play.

King Claudius. Give me some light. Step back.

Polonius. Lights, lights, lights!

[*Everyone exits except* Hamlet *and* Horatio.]

Hamlet. [*Sings*] *Let the wounded deer go weep.*
For some must watch while some must sleep.
Thus runs the world away.

The success of the play we just saw and a very fancy suit of clothes would make me an owner of a theater company.[17]

Horatio. Only a half owner.

Hamlet. A whole one. O good Horatio, I'll believe the ghost. Did you see?

Horatio. I saw, my lord.

Hamlet. When he talked about the poison?

Horatio. I saw him very well.

Hamlet. Ah ha! Come, some music!
[*Sings*] *For if the king likes not the comedy,*
Why then, perhaps he likes it not, by God!
Come, the recorders![18]

[*Enter* Rosencrantz *and* Guildenstern.]

Guildenstern. My Lord, may I have a word with you?

Hamlet. You may have a whole book.

Guildenstern. The king, sir—

Hamlet. Yes, sir, what about him?

Guildenstern. He is very upset.

---

[17] Shakespeare was a part owner in a theater company.
[18] recorders—wooden musical instruments like flutes.

Hamlet. With drink, sir?

Guildenstern. No, my lord, with anger.

Hamlet. You would be wiser to say this to a doctor, for if I tried to cure him I might make him angrier.

Guildenstern. Please, my lord, don't talk so wildly.

Hamlet. I am tame, sir. Speak.

Guildenstern. Your mother the queen is also very upset and has sent for you.

Hamlet. You are welcome.

Guildenstern. No, my good lord, that is not the right answer. If you would please answer me sanely, I will do what your mother asked. If not, I beg your pardon and ask you to let me leave.

Hamlet. Sir, I cannot.

Rosencrantz. What, my lord?

Hamlet. Answer you sanely. My mind is sick. But, sir, the best answer I can make, you shall take to my mother. Therefore, let's talk about it. My mother, you say—

Rosencrantz. She said that your actions have amazed and astonished her.

Hamlet. O wonderful son that can astonish a mother! But isn't there any more than an astonished mother? Tell me.

Rosencrantz. She wishes to speak to you privately before you go to bed.[19]

Hamlet. We would obey, even if she were ten times our mother. Do you have any other business with us?

Rosencrantz. My lord, you once thought I was your friend.

Hamlet. And still do.

Rosencrantz. Good my lord, why are you so upset? You are in danger of losing your own freedom if you cannot tell your friends your grief.[20]

Hamlet. Sir, I cannot advance.[21]

Rosencrantz. How can that be? The king, himself, has made it clear that you will be the next king.

---

[19] Rosencrantz and Guildenstern are starting Polonius's plan to listen to Hamlet and his mother speak in private.

[20] Rosencrantz is trying to warn Hamlet that the King might lock Hamlet up, or perhaps this is a threat.

[21] *Wordplay:* Hamlet cannot get a better position in life, because he should be king, but his uncle is king. Also Hamlet cannot move on with his plans for revenge.

Hamlet. Yes, sir, but "While the grass grows, the horse starves."[22] It is an old proverb. [*Musicians enter with recorders.*] O, the recorders. Let me see one. [*To* Rosencrantz *and* Guildenstern] Why are you trying to trap me?

Guildenstern. O my lord, I am only trying to be your friend. I didn't mean to upset you further.

Hamlet. I understand that. Here, play this recorder.

Guildenstern. My lord, I cannot.

Hamlet. Please, play it.

Guildenstern. Believe me, I don't know how.

Hamlet. It is as easy as lying. Cover these stops[23] with your fingers and thumb, blow into it, and you will have lovely music. Look, here are the stops.

Guildenstern. I cannot do this. I don't know how.

Hamlet. Then think how little you value *me*. You would play on me. You seem to know my stops. You would sound me from my lowest to my highest note. There is much music in me, but you cannot make it speak. God, do you think I

---

[22] While Hamlet's uncle is king, Hamlet cannot get what is his. Hamlet seems to be very honest and open here.

[23] stops—holes in the recorder.

am easier to play than a recorder? Call me what instrument you will, you cannot play me.

[*Enter* Polonius.]

God bless you, sir.

Polonius. My lord, the queen wishes to speak to you right away.

Hamlet. Do you see that cloud that looks like a camel?

Polonius. It does look like a camel.

Hamlet. I think it looks like a weasel.

Polonius. The top does look like a weasel.

Hamlet. Or like a whale.

Polonius. Very much like a whale.

Hamlet. Then I will go to my mother, before long. [*Aside*] I am sick of their tricks. [*To* Polonius] I will go, very soon.

Polonius. I will say so.

Hamlet. "Very soon" is easily said. Leave me, friends.

[*All but* Hamlet *exit.*]

'Tis now the very witching time[24] of night
When churchyards yawn[25] and hell itself
    breathes out
Evil to this world. Now I could drink hot blood
And do such terrible things that day
Would shake to see it. But now I will go to my
    mother.
I must remember to treat her as my mother.
Let me be cruel, but not unnatural.
I will speak daggers to her, but use none.
I will punish her with my words, not my
    deeds.

[Hamlet *exits.*]

---

[24] witching time—midnight, that time of night when witches come out.
[25] churchyards yawn—graves open.

ACT THREE, SCENE THREE

In a hall in Elsinore castle, Claudius orders Rosencrantz and Guildenstern to take Hamlet to England immediately. Polonius goes to spy on Hamlet and his mother. King Claudius, alone, admits that he killed his brother, the previous king. He tries to pray, but cannot. Hamlet comes in and wants to kill him immediately, but the king appears to be praying. Hamlet wants him to die when he is doing something sinful so that he will go to hell. So he decides to wait.

[*Enter* King Claudius, Rosencrantz, *and* Guildenstern.]

King Claudius. I do not like the way that Hamlet is acting. It's not safe to let his madness grow. Therefore get ready. I will send you both to England. And Hamlet shall go with you. His madness threatens us.

Guildenstern. We will get ready to leave. It is good to keep yourself safe when so many people depend on you.

Rosencrantz. All men want peace, but a king must seek peace for all his people. The peace of a kingdom depends on the peace of the king. When the king sighs, everyone groans.

King Claudius. Get ready for this speedy trip. We will imprison this fear that is now too free.

Rosencrantz. We will hurry.

[Rosencrantz *and* Guildenstern *exit. Enter* Polonius.]

Polonius. My Lord, he's going to his mother's room. I'll hide behind the curtain to hear what they say. I'm sure she will speak strongly to him. As you said (and wisely was it said, since nature makes mothers too kind), it's right that someone else should hear what is said. Fare you well, my lord. I'll visit you before you go to bed and tell you what I find out.

King Claudius. Thanks, my lord. [Polonius *exits.*]
O, my crime is rotten.[1] It smells to heaven.
It has the first and oldest curse on it—
A brother's murder.[2] I cannot pray.
Even though I really want to.

---

[1] Claudius, for the first time, is fully and clearly confessing the murder. He did it. The ghost was telling the truth.

[2] This is a reference to the Bible story of Cain who killed his brother Abel and became the first murderer.

My guilt is stronger than my good intentions.
Like a man who must work at two jobs,
I cannot decide what to do first,
So I don't do either one. What if this cursed hand
Was covered thickly with my brother's blood?
Is there not enough rain in the sweet heavens
To wash it white as snow? What is mercy for
Except to forgive sin? And what's in prayer
except to ask
That we be led away from sin,
Or, after we have sinned, to be forgiven?
Then I'll pray. My sin is past.
But, O, what prayer can help me?
"Forgive me my foul murder"?
That cannot be, since I still have
What I gained from murder:
My crown, my own ambition, and my queen.
Can I be pardoned and keep what I gained?
In this evil world, crime may escape justice,
And often what is gained by crime
Is used to escape the law.
But it is not so in heaven. There are no tricks
in heaven.
There the action is seen for what it is,
And we must give evidence against ourselves.

What then? What can I do?

Should I try to see what **repentance**[3] can and
    cannot do?

Yet what can repentance do when one can
    not repent?

O wretched state! O heart as dark as death!

O trapped soul, that, struggling to be free,

Is caught up more! Help, angels! Help with all
    your strength.

Bow, stubborn knees, and heart, as hard as steel,

Be as soft as a newborn baby!

All may be well.

[*He kneels to pray. Enter* Hamlet, *unseen and unheard
by the* king.]

Hamlet. Now might I kill him easily, while he is
    praying.

And now I'll do it. [*He draws his sword.*] And so
    he goes to heaven.

And is that my revenge? That needs to be
    thought about.

A villain kills my father. And for that,

I, his only son, send this same villain to heaven.

O, that would be reward, not revenge.

---

[3] **repentance**—true sorrow or regret for one's sins.

He killed my father when my father was fully
    enjoying this world,
With all his crimes unconfessed and unforgiven.
Who except heaven knows what my father
    must suffer for those crimes?
But will I be revenged if I kill him while he
    is praying?
When he is ready for death?
No!
I'll put away my sword and wait for a more
    horrible time.
I'll kill him when he is drunkenly asleep,
    or angry,
In incestuous pleasures, gambling, swearing,
Or doing something that will not help save
    his soul.
Then I'll trip him so that he falls headfirst
    into hell,
So that his soul may be as damned and black
As hell, where it is going.
My mother waits.
This medicine of praying only makes your
    sickly days a little longer.

[Hamlet *exits.*]

King Claudius. [*Standing up*] My words fly up. My thoughts remain below. Words without thoughts never go to heaven.[4]

[King Claudius *exits.*]

---

[4] Claudius is saying he wasn't really praying.

Polonius hides behind some curtains in the queen's bedroom to spy on Hamlet and the queen. Hamlet talks so wildly that the queen is afraid and cries out. Polonius also cries out. Hamlet thinks that the hidden Polonius is the king and stabs him to death through the curtain. Hamlet wildly accuses his mother of sinful behavior. The ghost returns and reminds Hamlet that he should not accuse his mother but should revenge his father's death. Queen Gertrude cannot see the ghost and pities Hamlet's madness. Hamlet suspects that the mission to England is a plot against him. He leaves, dragging Polonius's dead body.

[Queen Gertrude *and* Polonius *enter.*]

Polonius. He will come here right away. Speak strictly to him. Tell him his actions have been too much to put up with and that your majesty has protected him. I'll hide here. Please, speak plainly to him.

Hamlet. [*Offstage*] Mother, mother, mother!

Queen Gertrude. I'll do as you say. Fear not. Leave, I hear him coming.

[Polonius *hides behind the curtain. Enter* Hamlet.]

Hamlet. Now, mother, what's the matter?

Queen Gertrude. Hamlet, you have upset your father very much.

Hamlet. Mother, you have upset my father very much.

Queen Gertrude. Come, come, you answer foolishly.

Hamlet. Go, go, you speak wickedly.

Queen Gertrude. Why, what do you mean, Hamlet?

Hamlet. What's the matter now?

Queen Gertrude. Have you forgotten who I am?

Hamlet. No, by the cross, I haven't. You are the queen, your husband's brother's wife. And (I wish it wasn't so!) you are my mother.

Queen Gertrude. Nay, then, I'll call someone to come here that you *will* listen to.

Hamlet. Come, come, and sit you down. You shall not move. You will not go until I show you a mirror where you may see what you are really like.

Queen Gertrude. What will you do? Don't murder me. Help, help!

Polonius. [*Behind the curtains*] What! Help, help!

Hamlet. [*Drawing his sword*] How now! A rat? [Hamlet *stabs through the curtain.*] Dead. I'll bet a coin I've killed you!

Polonius. [*Behind*] O, I am killed! [*Falls and dies.*]

Queen Gertrude. O me, what have you done?

Hamlet. I don't know. Is it the king?

Queen Gertrude. O, what a foolish and bloody deed this is!

Hamlet. A bloody deed—almost as bad, good mother, as kill a king and marry his brother.

Queen Gertrude. As kill a king?

Hamlet. Yes, lady, that's what I said. [Hamlet *lifts up the curtain and discovers* Polonius.] You wretched, stupid, snooping fool, farewell! I thought you were someone better. Take what you get. Now you know it's dangerous to be too nosy. [*To his mother*] Stop wringing[1] your hands. Peace! Sit down, and let me wring your heart, for so I shall if it is soft enough. If your normal wickedness has not made it too hard for my words to reach.

Queen Gertrude. What have I done that you dare talk to me so rudely?

Hamlet. Such an act that makes modesty blush,
Makes goodness look false, makes innocent love
Look faded and sick, makes marriage promises
Into the lies of gamblers. O, you have taken the
  soul from marriage vows
And turned them into a senseless string
  of words.
The face of heaven blushes at the Earth
As if it were the end of the world. And heaven
Is sick at what has happened.

Queen Gertrude. Ay me, what has happened that is this terrible?

Hamlet. Look here, at this picture, and at this,
The picture of two brothers. [Hamlet *points to paintings of his father and uncle.*]

---

[1] wringing—twisting and squeezing.

See, what a grace was seated on this brow,

Hyperion's curls, the front of Jove himself,

An eye like Mars' to threaten and command.

A station like the herald Mercury

New-lighted on a heaven-kissing hill,

A combination and a form indeed

Where every god did seem to set his seal

To give the world assurance of a man.[2]

This was your husband. Look now at what
  follows.

Here is your new husband. He looks like
  something sick,

Making everything around him sick. Can
  you see?

How can you stop looking at this beautiful
  mountain and start looking at this desert?

Ha! Can you see? You cannot call it love.

At your age the passions are tamer and listen
  to good judgment.

And what judgment would tell you to go from
  this man to this man?

You can judge, but your judgment must be sick.

You aren't the slave of madness.

What devil was it that tricked you?

---

[2] Hamlet is comparing his father to the gods. Hyperion was the sun god, Jove the chief god, Mars the god of war, and Mercury the messenger of the gods. These eight lines are in Shakespeare's words.

Eyes without feeling, feeling without sight.
Ears without hands or eyes, smelling without all.
Even a sick part of one true sense could not be
    so stupid.
O shame! Where is your blush?
O passion, if you can cause a mature woman
To make such a bad choice,
Don't call it shameful when youthful passion
Acts without thought.

Queen Gertrude. O Hamlet, speak no more. You make me look deeply into my very soul, and there I see evil and deep stains that cannot be washed out.

Hamlet. Nay, but to live in the rotten sweat of a greasy bed, soaked in evil, making love in the nasty sty[3]—

Queen Gertrude. O, don't speak to me any more. These words, like daggers, enter my ears. No more, sweet Hamlet!

Hamlet. He is a murderer and a villain. He is not worth one twentieth of your first husband. He is the clown of kings. He has stolen his throne. He took the crown from a shelf and put it in his pocket—

---

[3] sty—place where pigs live.

Queen Gertrude. No more!

Hamlet. A king of shreds and patches—
[*Enter* the Ghost.] Save me, and hover over
me with your wings, you heavenly guards!
[*To the* Ghost.] What do you wish from me,
gracious figure?

Queen Gertrude. [Gertrude *can't see the* Ghost.]
Alas, he's mad!

Hamlet. [*To the* Ghost] Do you come to scold your son
because I have let time pass and passion cool
And have not carried out your dreadful
command?
O, tell me!

Ghost. Do not forget. This visit is to remind you what
you should be doing. But, look, your mother sits
in shock. O, step between her and her confused
soul. She is frightened. Speak to her, Hamlet.

Hamlet. Are you all right, lady?

Queen Gertrude. Alas, why are you looking and
talking to nothing? Your eyes stand out. Your
hair stands on end. O gentle son, please be calm.
What are you looking at?

Hamlet. At him, at him! Look how pale he stares
at us! His looks would make stones pay
attention. [*To the* Ghost] Do not look like that

unless you want me to feel pity instead of hunting for revenge. I will cry instead of shedding blood.

Queen Gertrude. To whom are you speaking?

Hamlet. Don't you see anything there?

Queen Gertrude. Nothing at all. Yet I see all that is there.

Hamlet. Did you hear anything?

Queen Gertrude. No, nothing but ourselves.

Hamlet. Why, look there! Look, how it walks away! It is my father, the way he looked when he lived! Look, there he goes, now, out the door!

[*The* Ghost *exits.*]

Queen Gertrude. This is your imagination. Your madness makes something out of nothing.

Hamlet. Madness? My pulse, like yours, is calm.
What I have said is not madness.
Test me. I will tell you what is wrong
In words that you will see are sane.
Mother, for love of grace, don't
Excuse your sins by saying that I'm mad.
This excuse would only hide the evil under it.
Confess yourself to heaven.
Repent what's past. Avoid what is to come.

Do not spread the compost[4] on the weeds, to
    make them grow.
Forgive my goodness, for in these evil times
Goodness must beg pardon of **vice**.[5]
Yes, goodness must bow to vice and beg to do
    him a favor.

Queen Gertrude. O Hamlet, you have broken my
    heart in two.

Hamlet. O, throw away the worse part of your heart,
    And live the purer with the other half.
    Good night—but do not go to my uncle's bed.
    Try to be virtuous, even if you're not.
    Bad habits create evil, but good habits create good.
    Do not go to his bed tonight,
    And that shall make it easier to stay away the
        next time.
    For habit can change our nature.
    Either ask the devil in, or throw him out.
    Once more, good night, and when you wish
        for God's blessing
    I'll ask for your blessing. For this lord,
    [*Pointing to* Polonius] I do repent.
    But heaven has planned it this way,
    To punish me with this and this with me

---

[4] compost—fertilizer.
[5] **vice**—evil.

That I must be the tool of God.

I will get rid of his body and will pay for his death.

So, again, good night.

I must be cruel in order to be kind.

Thus bad begins and worse is yet to come.

One word more, good lady.

Queen Gertrude. What shall I do?

Hamlet. Do not let the fat king tempt you again
    to bed,

Pet you, and call you his dear. Do not let him,

For a pair of filthy kisses,

Or stroking your neck with his fingers,

Make you to say that really I am not mad,

But mad in trickery. You would be good

Not to let him know. For who, except a queen
    who is fair, sober, wise,

Would hide such important matters from a toad,

From a bat, a witch's cat? Who would do so?

[*Sarcastically*] No, don't keep it a secret

But tell everything and destroy yourself.

Queen Gertrude. Be sure, if words are made
    of breath,

And breath of life, I have no life to breathe

What you have said to me.

Hamlet. I must go to England. Do you know that?

Queen Gertrude. Alas, I had forgotten. It has been decided.

Hamlet. There are letters sealed, and my
two schoolfellows,
Whom I will trust as I trust poisonous snakes,
Carry the official letter and command.
They must escort me and lead me into some
danger.
Let it work. It's good sport to have the bomber
hoist with his own petard.[6]
It will be difficult, but I will dig one yard
Below their mines, and blow them at the
moon. O, it is most sweet
When two plots meet. This man [*Looking at
Polonius's body*] shall start my plan.
I'll **lug**[7] the guts into the next room.
Mother, good night. Indeed this man
Is now most quiet, most secret, and
most serious,
Who was a chattering fool in life.
Come, sir, let's finish this business with you.
Good night, mother.

[*They exit in different directions.* Hamlet *drags
off* Polonius.]

---

[6] **hoist with his own petard**—blown up with his own explosives.
[7] **lug**—carry; drag.

In a room in Elsinore castle, Queen Gertrude reports Polonius's death to the king. King Claudius sends Rosencrantz and Guildenstern to find Hamlet and the dead body.

[*Enter* King Claudius, Queen Gertrude, Rosencrantz, *and* Guildenstern.]

King Claudius. There is a reason for these deep sighs. Tell me. It is right that we understand. Where is your son?

Queen Gertrude. [*To* Rosencrantz *and* Guildenstern] Please leave us alone for a while. [Rosencrantz *and* Guildenstern *exit.*] Ah, my lord, what I have seen tonight!

King Claudius. What, Gertrude? How is Hamlet?

Queen Gertrude. Mad as the sea and wind, when both fight over which is the stronger. In his uncontrollable fit, he heard something behind the arras. He whipped out his sword and cried, "A rat, a rat!" And, in this madness, he killed the hidden good old man.

King Claudius. O this is bad! If we had been hidden there, he would have killed us. His freedom is a threat to us all—to you, to us, to everyone. Alas, how shall I explain this bloody deed? We will be blamed for it. It was our duty to have kept this mad young man under control, away from people. But I cared for him so much that I didn't do what was needed. Where is he?

Queen Gertrude. Taking away the body he has killed. And this clearly shows his madness. He weeps for what he has done.

King Claudius. O Gertrude, come away! As soon as the sun rises over the mountains tomorrow morning, we will ship him away. We must, with our majesty and skill, both accept and excuse this horrible deed. Come here, Guildenstern!

[*Enter* Rosencrantz *and* Guildenstern.]

Friends both, go and find someone to help you. In his madness, Hamlet has killed Polonius and dragged the dead body away from his mother's room. Go find him. Speak carefully to Hamlet, and bring the body into the chapel. I pray you, do this quickly.

[*Exit* Rosencrantz *and* Guildenstern.]

Come, Gertrude, we'll call our wisest friends and let them know, both what we mean to do, and what has unfortunately been done. We will try to stop the gossip before it goes too far. O, come away! My soul is full of anger and sorrow.

[*They exit.*]

In another room in the castle, Hamlet refuses to tell Rosencrantz and Guildenstern where the body is.

[*Enter* Hamlet.]

Hamlet. Safely hidden.

Rosencrantz. [*Offstage*] Hamlet! Lord Hamlet!

Hamlet. What's that noise? Who calls on Hamlet? O, here they come.

[*Enter* Rosencrantz *and* Guildenstern.]

Rosencrantz. What have you done, my lord, with the dead body?

Hamlet. Mixed it with dust, to which it is related.

Rosencrantz. Tell us where it is, so we may take it to the chapel.

Hamlet. Do not believe it.

Rosencrantz. Believe what?

Hamlet. That I can keep your secret and not my own. Besides, when questioned by a sponge, what answer should a king's son give?

Rosencrantz. Do you think I am a sponge, my lord?

Hamlet. Yes, sir. You are a sponge that soaks up the king's favors, his rewards, his orders. Such servants do the king their best service in the end. He keeps them like an ape keeps an apple in the corner of his jaw. First he holds it carefully, to be at last swallowed. When he needs what you have found out, he will squeeze you, and, sponge, you shall be dry again.

Rosencrantz. I don't understand you, my lord.

Hamlet. I am glad. A sarcastic speech is wasted on fools.

Rosencrantz. My lord, you must tell us where the body is, and go with us to the king.

Hamlet. The body is with the king, but the king is not with the body. The king is a thing[1]—

Guildenstern. "A thing," my lord?

Hamlet. A nothing. Take me to him.

---

[1] Hamlet's "mad" answer might mean that Polonius is in the castle with the king, but the king is not dead with Polonius.

In another room in the castle, Hamlet finally tells the king where he has hidden Polonius's body. King Claudius sends Hamlet on a trip to England that day. Once alone, King Claudius says that he will have Hamlet murdered in England.

[*Enter* King Claudius, *with* Attendants.]

King Claudius. I have sent to find him, and to find the body. It is dangerous that this man is free! Yet we must not use the strong law on him. He's loved by the unsettled crowd who don't choose with their minds, but with their eyes. And where this is true, they criticize the punishment and never think of the crime. So that everything goes smoothly, his sudden departure must seem part of a plan. Serious diseases are cured by serious treatment, or are not cured at all.

[*Enter* Rosencrantz.]

How now! What has happened?

Rosencrantz. He will not tell us where he has hidden the body, my lord.

King Claudius. But where is he?

Rosencrantz. Outside, my lord, under guard, waiting to know what you wish to do with him.

King Claudius. Bring him before us.

Rosencrantz. Guildenstern! Bring in the lord.

[*Enter* Hamlet *and* Guildenstern.]

King Claudius. Now, Hamlet, where's Polonius?

Hamlet. At supper.

King Claudius. At supper where?

Hamlet. Not where he eats, but where he is eaten. A certain meeting of polite worms are eating him. A worm eats better than a king. We fatten all creatures to fatten us, and we fatten ourselves for worms. Your fat king and your lean beggar are but different dishes at a meal, two dishes, but for one table. That's the end of us all.

King Claudius. Alas, alas!

Hamlet. A man may fish with the worm that has eaten on a king, and then eat the fish that has fed on that worm.

King Claudius. What do you mean by this?

Hamlet. Nothing but to show you how a king may go on a trip through the guts of a beggar.

King Claudius. Where is Polonius?

Hamlet. In heaven. Send for him there. If your messenger doesn't find him there, search for him in the other place yourself. But indeed, if you don't find him this month, you shall smell him as you go up the stairs into the lobby.

King Claudius. [*To* Attendants] Go, search for him there.

Hamlet. He will wait until you come.

[Attendants *exit.*]

King Claudius. Hamlet, for this action, we must quickly send you away from here, for your own safety—which we deeply care for, as we are deeply sorry for what you have done. Therefore get yourself ready. The ship is ready, and the wind is in the right direction. Your friends are waiting for you, and everything is ready for you to go to England.

Hamlet. To England?

King Claudius. Yes, Hamlet.

Hamlet. Good.

King Claudius. So is it, if you knew why we send you.

Hamlet. I see an angel that knows why.[1] But, come, I'll go to England! Farewell, dear mother.

King Claudius. I am your loving father, Hamlet.

Hamlet. My mother. Father and mother are man and wife. Man and wife are one flesh. And so, "my mother." Come, to England!

[Hamlet *exits.*]

King Claudius. Follow him closely. Get him on board the ship quickly. Don't delay. I want him gone tonight. Away! Everything is taken care of. [*All but* King Claudius *exit.*] And, England,[2] if

---

[1] Here Hamlet hints that the angels know Claudius's reason for sending him to England. It is to have him killed.

[2] England—Claudius is addressing the King of England.

you want my friendship—as my great power may make you do, since you still pay us tribute and know our military power—you may not lightly ignore what we ask for in the letters we send you. We want the immediate death of Hamlet. Do it, England, for he is like a fever in my blood, and you must cure me. Until I know it is done, whatever my fortune, I cannot be happy until then.

[King Claudius *exits.*]

On a plain in Demark, Hamlet meets the young Norwegian Prince Fortinbras. He is marching through Denmark on his way to fight in Poland. Hamlet compares Fortinbras's action with his own lack of action. He decides to move faster toward revenging his father's death.

[*Enter* Fortinbras, *a* Captain, *and* Soldiers, *marching.*]

Prince Fortinbras. Go, captain, send my greetings to the Danish king. Tell him that, with his permission, Fortinbras is ready to lead the Norwegian army through Denmark. If the king wishes to speak with us, tell him we will pay our respects to him personally.

Captain. I will do it, my Lord.

Prince Fortinbras. Go quietly on.

[*Exit* Fortinbras *and* Soldiers. *Enter* Hamlet, Rosencrantz, Guildenstern, *and others.*]

Hamlet. Good sir, whose soldiers are these?

Captain. They are from Norway, sir.

Hamlet. Where are they going, sir?

Captain. To fight in some part of Poland.

Hamlet. Who commands them, sir?

Captain. The nephew to the old king of Norway, Fortinbras.

Hamlet. Are they attacking Poland itself, or some Polish territory?

Captain. To speak truly, and with no exaggeration, we go to gain a little piece of ground that will not do us any good except that we will be called conquerors. I would not pay five ducats[1] in rent to farm it. Nor would it give Norway or Poland any more money if it were sold.

Hamlet. Why, then the Poles never will defend it.

Captain. Yes, it is already defended with an army.

Hamlet. Two thousand lives and twenty thousand ducats will not settle who gets this worthless

---

[1] ducats—coins.

piece of land. This is the hidden **abscess**[2] of much wealth and peace, that, without being seen, bursts and causes the man to die. I humbly thank you, sir.

Captain. God be with you, sir. [*The* Captain *exits.*]

Rosencrantz. Will it please you to leave now, my lord?

Hamlet. I'll be with you right away. Go on ahead
a little. [*Exit all except* Hamlet.]
All things seem to remind me
That I must revenge my father's death!
What is a man, if all he does with his time
Is sleep and eat? A beast, no more.
God, who made us so intelligent,
Able to learn from the past and plan for
the future,
Didn't give us that ability and godlike reason
To rot in us unused. Now, maybe it is
Mindlessness like the beasts'
Or some cowardly hesitation
That results from thinking too much about
the action.

---

[2] **abscess**—sore filled with pus.

I do not know why I still live to say
"This thing's to be done,"
Since I have a reason, and wish, and strength
and ability
To do it. Examples as obvious as the Earth tell
me to do it.
Witness this army of such size and expense
Led by a sensitive and young prince,
Whose spirit is filled with divine ambition.
He doesn't worry about what might happen.
He exposes life and fortune to all that luck,
death, and danger
Dare him to do, even for something that's
unimportant.
To be truly great, a person must not be willing
to fight
Without a great cause, unless honor is at risk.
What about me then? I have a father killed,
A mother stained. I have good reasons
To do this, and I don't do anything.
While, to my shame, I see the approaching death
Of twenty thousand men, that, for a daydream
And the **illusion**[3] of fame, go to their graves
Like they would go to their beds.

---

[3] **illusion**—a false understanding of reality.

They are going to fight for a piece of land
That is not big enough for them to stand on
    when they fight
Or be buried in when they are killed. O, from
    now on,
My thoughts will be bloody or be worth nothing!

[Hamlet *exits.*]

In a room in Elsinore castle, a gentleman of the court tells Gertrude that Ophelia has gone mad. Ophelia sings about death and betrayal. King Claudius is upset because he fears Ophelia's brother Laertes. Laertes has returned from France and wants to revenge the death of his father Polonius. Laertes invades the king's rooms with a group of people who wish to make Laertes king. Ophelia appears again, having obviously gone mad. King Claudius tells Laertes to ask some friends to find out what happened.

[*Enter* Queen Gertrude, Horatio, *and a* Gentleman.]

Queen Gertrude. I will not speak with her.

Gentleman. She will not stop asking. She is **distraught.**[1] She is to be pitied.

---

[1] **distraught**—distracted; mentally unstable; crazy.

Queen Gertrude. What does she want?

Gentleman. She speaks much of her father. She says she hears there are plots in the world. Then she sits and thinks and beats her heart. She gets upset at small things. She says things that don't make sense or only half make sense. Her speech is meaningless, yet her pitiful condition makes the hearers draw conclusions. They try to understand her, but in the end they put her words together to fit their own thoughts. Her winks, and nods, and gestures make one think there might be some unhappy meaning to what she says, though nothing certain.

Horatio. It is best to speak with her. She may give bad ideas to some troublemakers.

Queen Gertrude. Let her come in. [*Exit* Horatio.] [*Aside*] To my sin-sick soul, each small thing seems the beginning of some great problem. So full of clumsy suspicion is my guilt that I might spill everything and destroy myself out of fear of being destroyed.

[*Enter* Horatio, *with* Ophelia.]

Ophelia. Where is the beautiful queen of Denmark?

Queen Gertrude. How are you, Ophelia!

Ophelia. [*Sings[2]*] *How should I your true love know*
　　From another one?
　By his shell-like hat and staff,
　　And his sandal shoes.[3]

Queen Gertrude. Alas, sweet lady, what do you mean?

Ophelia. What did you say? No, listen.
　[*Sings*] *He is dead and gone, lady.*
　　He is dead and gone.
　At his head green grass, at his heels a stone.

Queen Gertrude. No, but Ophelia—

Ophelia. Pray you, listen.
　[*Sings*] *White is his **shroud**[4] as the mountain snow—*

[*Enter* King Claudius.]

Queen Gertrude. Alas, look here, my lord.

Ophelia. [*Sings*] *Covered with sweet flowers*
　　Which did not go to the grave
　Covered with tears, with true-love tears.

---

[2] Ophelia has gone mad over the death of her father and the loss of her "true love," Hamlet. Perhaps what has truly driven her mad is the sudden and complete destruction of her innocence. She sings a lot, mostly small pieces of old songs. Her speech does not always make sense.

[3] Ophelia's description of the lover's clothes fits the description of the clothes of a religious pilgrim.

[4] **shroud**—cloth a dead body was wrapped in.

King Claudius. How are you, pretty lady?

Ophelia. Well. May God reward you! In stories they say a baker's daughter was turned into an owl for punishment. Lord, we know what we are, but don't know what we may be. God be at your table!

King Claudius. This must be about her father.

Ophelia. Pray you, let's not talk about this, but when they ask you what it means, say this:
[*Sings*] *To-morrow is Saint Valentine's day,*
    All in the early morning,
And I am a maid[5] at your window,
    To be your Valentine.
Then up he rose, and put on his clothes,
    And opened the bedroom door.
He let in the maid, that out a maid
    Never departed more.

King Claudius. Pretty Ophelia—

Ophelia. Indeed, without saying anything bad, I'll end this song.
[*Sings*] *By Jesus and by Saint Charity,*
    Alack, and fie for shame!
Young men will do it if they come to it.

---

[5] *maid*—innocent girl; virgin.

> *By God, they are to blame.*
> *Said she, before you ruined me,*
> > *You promised me to wed.*
> *He replied,*
> > *So would I have done, by yonder sun,*
> *If you hadn't come to my bed.*

King Claudius. How long has she been this way?

Ophelia. I hope all will be well. We must be patient, but I cannot help weeping, to think they shall lay him in the cold ground. My brother shall know of it.[6] And so I thank you for your good advice. Come, my coach! Good night, ladies, good night, sweet ladies. Good night, good night.

[Ophelia *exits.*]

King Claudius. Follow her closely. Watch her carefully, I pray you.
[*Exit* Horatio.]
O, this is the poison of deep grief.
It comes from her father's death.
O Gertrude, Gertrude,
When sorrows come, they don't come alone.
They come in armies. First, her father is killed.
Next, your son leaves. He violently caused his
own removal.

---

[6] She will tell her brother about the death of their father, Polonius.

The people are confused.

They are thinking and whispering about good
     Polonius's death.

We have been foolish

To bury him quickly and secretly.

Poor Ophelia. She has lost her mind.

Without it, we are animals.

Last, and just as serious,

Her brother secretly came from France.

He is very confused and suspicious.

He stays away from us.

And many people tell him the worst.

They need to blame someone and, lacking facts,

They say this is all my fault.

O my dear Gertrude, this army of troubles kills
     me over and over.

[*A noise offstage*]

Queen Gertrude. Alas, what noise was that?

King Claudius. Where are my guards? Guard the
door. [*Enter a* Messenger.] What's the matter?

Messenger. Save yourself, my lord. The ocean
doesn't flood the lowlands faster than young
Laertes[7] overcomes your guards. The people call

---

[7] Laertes is Ophelia's brother and Polonius's son. He has returned from
France after hearing about his father's death.

him lord. And, as if they wanted to start a new world, forgetting law and tradition, they cry "We choose Laertes to be king."[8] They throw their caps in the air, cheer, and applaud, shouting "Laertes shall be king, Laertes king!"

[*More noise offstage*]

Queen Gertrude. They are like happy dogs barking at the wrong trail! O, this is wrong, you false Danish dogs!

King Claudius. They've broken down the doors.

[*Enter* Laertes *and* Laertes's Followers.]

Laertes. Where is this king? [*To the crowd of his supporters*] Sirs, wait outside for me.

Laertes's Followers. No, we'll come in.

Laertes. I pray you, do as I ask.

Laertes's Followers. We will. We will.

Laertes. I thank you. Guard the door.
[Laertes's Followers *exit*.]
 O you evil king. Give me my father!

Queen Gertrude. Calmly, good Laertes.

---

[8] The king of Denmark was elected by the people. The old king would name a new one, but the people then voted to accept or reject the old king's choice.

Laertes. No true son would be calm about his father's murder. That drop of blood that's calm would prove that my mother was not true to my father.

[Gertrude *tries to stop* Laertes.]

King Claudius. What is the cause of this violence, Laertes?—Let him go, Gertrude. Do not fear he will hurt us. God protects a king.—Tell me, Laertes, why are you so angry?—Let him go, Gertrude.—Speak, man.

Laertes. Where is my father?

King Claudius. Dead.

Queen Gertrude. But the king did not kill him.

King Claudius. Let him ask what he wishes.

Laertes. How did he die? I'll not be lied to. My loyalty to a king can go to hell! Conscience and grace can go to the deepest pit of hell! I dare damnation. The only thing that matters is that I will revenge my father.

King Claudius. Who shall stop you?

Laertes. No one! I will use what little power I have to do this one thing.

King Claudius. Good Laertes, in your desire to know what happened to your father, must you destroy friends as well as enemies?

Laertes. I will only destroy his enemies.

King Claudius. Do you know them, then?

Laertes. To his good friends I'll open my arms wide. I'll die for them!

King Claudius. Why, now you speak like a good son and a true gentleman. I am not guilty of your father's death, and I am very sorry for it. You shall see this as clearly as you see daylight.

Laertes's Followers. [*Offstage*] Let her in.

Laertes. How now! What noise is that?

[*Enter* Ophelia.]

O heat, dry up my brains! Salt tears burn out my eyes![9] [*To* Ophelia] By heaven, your madness shall be paid for. O rose of May! Dear maid, kind sister, sweet Ophelia! O heavens, is it possible that a young girl's mind should be as **mortal**[10] as an old man's life? Her mind has gone with our dead father.

---

[9] Laertes would rather go mad and blind than see his sister in this condition.

[10] **mortal**—able to die.

Ophelia. [*Sings*] *They carried him barefaced to his grave.*

> *Hey non nonny, nonny, hey nonny.*[11]
> *And in his grave rained many a tear.*

Fare you well, my dove!

Laertes. If you were sane and tried to talk me into revenge, you could not offer a better reason than this.

Ophelia. You must sing "A-down a-down, and you, call him a-down-a." It is the false servant, that stole his master's daughter.

Laertes. This nonsense says more than sense could say.

Ophelia. [*Handing out real or imaginary flowers.*[12]] There's rosemary, that's for remembrance. Pray, love, remember. There's pansies. That's for thoughts.

Laertes. A lesson in madness, thoughts and remembrance for our father.

---

[11] These are nonsense words in a song, like *tra la la.*

[12] Ophelia will give presents of flowers and herbs. In Shakespeare's time each plant stood for something. Ophelia tells us that *rosemary* is for remembrance, *pansies* for thoughts, *fennel* for flattery, *columbines* for cheating in marriage, *rue* for repentance, *daisies* for unhappy love, and *violets* for faithfulness.

Ophelia. There's fennel for you, and columbines. There's rue for you, and here's some for me. There's a daisy. I would give you some violets, but they all withered when my father died. They say he made a good end.

[*Sings*] *For bonny sweet Robin is all my joy.*

Laertes. Thought and sorrow, suffering, hell itself, she makes these seem pretty.

Ophelia. [*Sings*] *And will he not come again?*
And will he not come again?
    No, no, he is dead.
    Go to your deathbed.
He never will come again.

His beard was as white as snow.
He is gone. He is gone.
    And we waste our grief.
    God have mercy on his soul!
And on all Christian souls, I pray God. God be with you.

[Ophelia *exits.*]

Laertes. Do you see this, O God?

King Claudius. Laertes, I must share in your grief. Come here for a moment. Choose some of your wisest friends. They shall hear and judge what I have to tell you. We will give you our kingdom, our crown, our life, everything we have if they find us in any way guilty. But if we are not guilty, be patient, and we will help to make things right.

Laertes. Let this be so. How did he die? Why was his funeral a secret? Why wasn't a marker raised over his grave? Why wasn't his funeral performed with all the honor he deserved? These questions cry out to heaven and Earth for an answer. I must have an answer to these questions.

King Claudius. So you shall. And let the ax fall on the guilty. I pray you, go with me.

[*They exit.*]

In another room in the castle, Horatio receives a letter from Hamlet saying that pirates attacked his ship on the way to England and brought him back, a prisoner, to Denmark.

[*Enter* Horatio *and a* Servant.]

Horatio. Who wishes to speak with me?

Servant. Sailors, sir. They say they have letters for you.

Horatio. Let them come in. [*Exit* Servant.] I do not know who should be sending me letters from abroad except Lord Hamlet.

[*Enter* Sailors.]

First Sailor. God bless you, sir.

Horatio. Let him bless you too.

First Sailor. He shall, sir, if it please him. There's a letter for you, sir, if your name is Horatio, as I am told it is. It comes from the ambassador that was going to England.

Horatio. [*Reads*] *Horatio, read this, then take these fellows to the king. They have letters for him.*

Before we were two days at sea, a very warlike pirate chased us. Finding ourselves too slow, we had to fight. In the fight, I got on the pirate's ship. At that moment, they got clear of our ship, so I alone became their prisoner.

They have treated me like kind thieves. But they know what they are doing. I am to do a favor for them. Let the king have the letters I have sent, and come to me as quickly as you would run away from death.

I will tell you something unbelievable. These good fellows will bring you to me. Rosencrantz and Guildenstern are still heading for England. I have much to tell you about them. Farewell.

Your friend, Hamlet.

Come, I will help you with your business. And do it quickly so that you may take me to the man who sent these letters.

[*They exit.*]

In another room in the castle, King Claudius receives the news that Hamlet has returned. King Claudius has told Laertes that Hamlet is guilty. He gets Laertes's help to kill Hamlet. Laertes will fence—have a sport fight with swords—with Hamlet, but he will poison the point of his sword. If Laertes fails, King Claudius will offer Hamlet some poisoned wine. Queen Gertrude enters to tell them that Ophelia in her madness has drowned.

[*Enter* King Claudius *and* Laertes.]

King Claudius. Now you know that I am not guilty, since you see that the man who murdered your father was trying to murder me.

Laertes. It is clear, but tell me why you didn't punish him. His crime and the threat to your life deserved his death.

King Claudius. O, for two special reasons. They may, perhaps, seem weak to you. But to me they are strong. The queen his mother loves him deeply, and for myself—my goodness or my great misfortune, whichever it is—I love her so much that I could not hurt her. The other reason? The people love him so much that they would not let me harm him in any way.

Laertes. So I have lost a noble father and have a sister driven into madness. She was worth more than any other person I know of. If nothing else, I will revenge her.

King Claudius. Don't lose sleep over that. You must not think that we are so weak that we can be threatened and not do anything about it. You shortly shall hear more. I loved your father, and we love ourself. And that, I hope, will teach you to imagine—[*Enter a* Messenger.] What now! What news?[1]

Messenger. Letters, my lord, from Hamlet. These to your majesty. This to the queen.

King Claudius. From Hamlet! Who brought them?

---

[1] Claudius is expecting news from England about Hamlet, but not the news he is about to get.

Messenger. Sailors, my lord, but I didn't see them. They were given to me by Claudio. He received them from the man who brought them.

King Claudius. Laertes, you shall hear them. Leave us.

[*Exit* Messenger.]

[*Reads*] *"High and mighty, you shall know I am in your kingdom alone and without money, without anything. To-morrow I shall beg to see your kingly eyes. Then I shall, first asking your pardon for it, tell why I have suddenly and strangely returned. Hamlet."*

What does this mean? Have all the rest come back? Or is it some trick, and no one has returned?

Laertes. Do you recognize the writing?

King Claudius. It's Hamlet's writing. "Without anything!" And "alone." What does this mean?

Laertes. I don't understand it, my lord. But let him come. It warms the sickness in my heart to know that I shall live and tell him to his face, "You did it."

King Claudius. If it be so, Laertes. (But how could it be so? But how could it be otherwise?) Will you take my advice?

Laertes. Yes, my lord, if you will not advise me to forget my search for revenge and make peace.

King Claudius. Your own peace. If he has returned, and doesn't mean to go on this trip, I have a plan to take care of him. No one will blame us for his death, and even his mother will think it an accident.

Laertes. My lord, I will do as you say. But I would like to be the one to kill him.

King Claudius. It is right. While you have been out of the country, people have talked about something you can do. It has made Hamlet jealous.

Laertes. What was it, my lord?

King Claudius. A youthful sport, but useful too. There was a gentleman who visited here from Normandy in France. He was the best rider I have ever seen. He and his horse did wonderful things as if he and the horse were a single being.

Laertes. A Norman?

King Claudius. A Norman.

Laertes. Upon my life, it must have been Lamond.

King Claudius. The very same man.

Laertes. I know him well. He is the best on horseback in all France.

King Claudius. He talked about you and said you were very good with the sword. He cried out that you could beat anyone in France. Sir, this report of his made Hamlet so envious that all he could do was wish and beg for your return to Denmark so that he could fence[2] with you. Now, out of this—

Laertes. What of this, my lord?

King Claudius. Laertes, was your father dear to you? Or are you like the painting of a sorrow, a face without a heart?

Laertes. Why do you ask this?

King Claudius. It is not that I think you did not love your father, but that I know love changes. And I have seen proof of that. Time can make love stronger or weaker. We should do what we wish when we wish it. For what we wish to do changes. Many things change what we wish to do. And then this "should do" often makes us feel bad as we think about it. But, to the center of the problem—Hamlet comes back. What will you do to show yourself your father's son in actions, not just in words?

Laertes. Cut his throat in the church.

---

[2] fence—fight (as a sport) with swords. Claudius is flattering Laertes and lying about Hamlet's jealousy to get Laertes to do what he, Claudius, wishes.

King Claudius. Indeed, no place should protect a murderer. Revenge should have no limits. But, good Laertes, will you do this? Stay in your rooms. When Hamlet returns, he shall know you are home. We'll have some people praise your skill with the sword and double the praise the Frenchman gave you. We'll set up a match between you. And we'll bet on who will win. He, being carelessly trusting, very generous, and without any trickery,[3] will not check the swords. With ease, or with a little trickery, you may choose a sword with the button[4] removed, and in a treacherous thrust pay him back for your father.

Laertes. I will do it. And, for that purpose, I'll dunk the tip of my sword in a powerful, deadly poison. Where it touches blood, nothing can save the thing it touches from death. With *this* poison, it means death even if he is just scratched.

King Claudius. Let's think about this. What is the best time to do this? If this should fail, and he sees what we are doing, it would be better not to do it. We need to have another plan in case this fails. Wait! Let me see. We'll make a large bet on

---

[3] Claudius is praising Hamlet! This does not fit with what he is telling Laertes, but it is the truth. However, Laertes is too upset to realize he is being tricked.

[4] In the sport of fencing, the sword has a button on its point, so it will not hurt anyone. The king is suggesting removing that button.

your skill. I have it! When in the fight you both are hot and dry, and he calls for a drink, I'll have prepared a cup of wine for him. If he drinks that wine, we will have no further worry about him. Who is coming?

[*Enter* Queen Gertrude.]

What's wrong, sweet queen!

Queen Gertrude. One sorrow comes fast after another. Your sister's drowned, Laertes.

Laertes. Drowned! O, where?[5]

Queen Gertrude. There is a willow tree that grows across a stream. This tree hangs its pale leaves in the glassy stream. There Ophelia covered a willow wreath with crowflowers, nettles, daisies, and orchids, which our cold maids call "dead man's fingers." She climbed up to put the wreath on a branch, which broke. Then she and the weedy wreath fell into the brook. Her clothes spread wide and, mermaid-like, they kept her afloat for a while. In that time, she sang bits of old songs as if she didn't realize her own danger, or as if she were a creature who lives in the water. But soon her clothes became heavy

---

[5] Shakespeare expects the actor to deliver these lines so that we see how upset Laertes really is.

with water and pulled the poor sad girl from her singing to a muddy death.

Laertes. Alas, then, she is drowned?

Queen Gertrude. Drowned, drowned.

Laertes. You have already had too much water, poor Ophelia, and therefore I will not cry. But yet, it is only natural, even if we try not to. [*He cries.*] When these tears are finished, I will be a man again. Adieu, my lord. I have a speech of fire that wants to burn, but these tears have put it out.

[Laertes *exits.*]

King Claudius. Let's follow, Gertrude. It was very hard for me to calm his anger! Now I fear this will start it again. Therefore, let's follow.

[*They exit.*]

ACT FIVE, SCENE ONE

In a churchyard, Hamlet and Horatio overhear two
gravediggers digging a grave. Hamlet asks the gravediggers
who they have buried. A priest comes into the churchyard,
followed by mourners with Ophelia's body. Laertes jumps
into the grave and demands to be buried with Ophelia.
He says that Hamlet caused her death. Hearing this,
Hamlet shows himself. Laertes attacks Hamlet. Hamlet
says he loved Ophelia more than anyone else did.

[*Enter two* Gravediggers, *with shovels.*[1]]

First Gravedigger. Is she to be buried in a
    Christian cemetery when she took her own life?[2]

---

[1] In the middle of this tragedy, Shakespeare gives his audience a little dark
humor from the two comic gravediggers.

[2] The gravediggers are suggesting that Ophelia committed suicide. If that were
true, according to the church law of the time, she could not be buried in a
Christian cemetery.

Second Gravedigger. I tell you she is, and therefore dig her grave right away. The crowner[3] has sat on her, and says she may have a Christian burial.

First Gravedigger. How can that be, unless she drowned herself in her own defense?

Second Gravedigger. Why, that's what they said.

First Gravedigger. It must be *se offendendo*.[4] It cannot be anything else. For here lies the point: if I drown myself knowingly, it argues an act, and an act has three parts—it is to act, to do, to perform. Argal,[5] she drowned herself knowingly.

Second Gravedigger. Nay, but listen, goodman digger—

First Gravedigger. Let me go on. Here lies the water, good. Here stands the man, good. If the man go to this water and drown himself, it is (will he, nill he[6]) he goes. Remember that. But if the water comes to him and drowns him, he doesn't

---

[3] *Wordplay:* crowner—coroner. The coroner, an official who rules on the cause of death, sat on or held a hearing about Ophelia's death. He did not sit on her!

[4] The real legal term is *se defendendo*, Latin for "in self-defense." The gravedigger is trying to sound like a lawyer.

[5] Argal—The real Latin term here is *ergo*, which means "therefore."

[6] will he, nill he—willy-nilly, whether he wants to or not.

drown himself. Argal, he that is not guilty of his own death doesn't shorten his own life.

Second Gravedigger. But is this law?

First Gravedigger. Yes, marry, it is the crowner's law.

Second Gravedigger. Do you want to know the truth? If this had not been a gentlewoman,[7] she would not have been given a Christian burial.

First Gravedigger. So that's the truth. And the more is the pity that in this world great folk should be able to drown or hang themselves more than their fellow Christians. Give me my shovel. The oldest gentlemen are gardeners, ditch diggers, and grave-makers. They work at Adam's[8] profession.

Second Gravedigger. Was he a gentleman?

First Gravedigger. He was the first that ever bore arms.[9]

Second Gravedigger. Why, he didn't have any.

---

[7] gentlewoman—upper-class or rich woman.

[8] Adam's—that of Adam, the first man, according to the Bible.

[9] bore arms—had a coat of arms. *Wordplay:* this is a pun on *arms* as a part of the body and also the coat of arms, or symbol of a noble family.

First Gravedigger. What, are you a **heathen?**[10] Don't you understand the Bible? The Bible says "Adam digged." Could he dig without arms? I'll ask you another question. If you can't answer it, admit I know more than you—

Second Gravedigger. Go on.

First Gravedigger. Who is he that builds stronger than either the stone worker, the shipbuilder, or the carpenter?

Second Gravedigger. The gallows-maker.[11] That frame outlives a thousand people who hang on it.

First Gravedigger. You're pretty smart. In good faith, the gallows is a good answer, but how is it a good answer? It is a good answer to those that do bad. Now you do bad to say the gallows is built stronger than the church. Argal, the gallows may be good for you. Try again, come on.

Second Gravedigger. "Who builds stronger than a stone worker, a shipbuilder, or a carpenter?"

First Gravedigger. Yes, tell me that, and let's stop working.

---

[10] **heathen**—someone who doesn't believe what you believe. In this case, a non-Christian.

[11] gallows-maker—one who builds the wooden structure used to hang a person in an execution.

Second Gravedigger. Marry, now I can tell.

First Gravedigger. Tell.

Second Gravedigger. By the Mass, I cannot tell.

[*Enter Hamlet and* Horatio, *at a distance.*]

First Gravedigger. Don't beat your brains any more about it, for your dull ass will not go any faster when it's beaten. When you are asked this question again, say "a grave-maker." The houses that he makes last until doomsday.[12] Go, get me a drink. Bring me a big glass of beer.
[*The* Second Gravedigger *exits. The* First Gravedigger *continues to dig. He starts to sing.*]
In youth, when I did love, did love,
*   I thought it was very sweet*
To pass—O,[13] the time, for, ah, my own good.
*   O, I thought there—ah—was nothing—ah—*
*   better.*

Hamlet. Has this fellow no feeling for his business, that he sings at grave-making?

Horatio. He is used to it.

Hamlet. That's true. He would feel it more if he hadn't done it so much.

---

[12] doomsday—the end of the world.

[13] The gravedigger says "O" and "ah" because he is working hard as he sings.

First Gravedigger. [*Sings*] *But age, with his*
stealing steps,
Has grabbed me with his claws,
And has made me old,
As if I had never been young.

[*The* Gravedigger *digs up a skull.*]

Hamlet. That skull had a tongue in it and could sing once. How he throws the jawbone to the ground, as if it were Cain's[14] jawbone, who did the first murder! It might be the head of a politician, which this ass[15] now gets the better of, one that could cheat God. Couldn't it be?

Horatio. It might, my lord.

Hamlet. Or of a member of the royal court, who could say "Good morning, sweet lord! How are you, good lord?" This might be my lord so-and-so, that praised my lord such-a-one's horse, when he meant to make fun of it. Might it not?

Horatio. Yes, my lord.

---

[14] In the Bible, Cain killed his brother Abel. Hamlet is thinking about King Claudius who killed his own brother.

[15] ass—fool.

Hamlet. Why, it could be, and now it belongs to my Lady Worm.[16] Now he doesn't have a jaw and is hit on the head with a gravedigger's shovel. Here's a fine change if we were able to see it. Did these bones[17] live only so they could end up being tossed around as if they were in a game. My bones ache to think about it.

First Gravedigger. [*Singing*]
A pick-axe, and a shovel, a spade
And a sheet to wrap a body in.
O, a pit of clay to be made
For such a guest is right.

[*He digs up another skull.*]

Hamlet. There's another. Might that be the skull of a lawyer? Where are his arguments now, his hair-splitting definitions, his cases, his deeds, and his tricks? Why does he allow this rude knave[18] to knock him on the head with a dirty shovel and does not tell him it's against the law? Hum! This fellow might have been, when he was alive, a great buyer of land, with his fines and his complicated legal tricks. Is this what he

---

[16] Lady Worm—creature who lives in the earth and was said to eat the remains of buried bodies.

[17] *Wordplay:* In Shakespeare's time, dice were called bones.

[18] knave—low-class man.

must finally pay for his land? To have his fine head full of fine dirt? Is that all the land he finally gets? A deed wouldn't fit in this [Hamlet *points to the skull.*] box, and that's all he has?

Horatio. Nothing more, my lord.

Hamlet. Is not parchment[19] made of sheepskins?

Horatio. Yes, my Lord, and of calfskins too.

Hamlet. Those who think a deed gives them anything are sheep and calves.[20] I will speak to this fellow. [*To the* Gravedigger] Whose grave is this, sirrah?[21]

First Gravedigger. Mine, sir.
[*Singing*] *O, a pit of clay to be made*
For such a guest is right.

Hamlet. I think it be yours, indeed, for you lie[22] in it.

First Gravedigger. You lie out of it, sir, and therefore it is not yours. For my part, I do not lie in it, and yet it is mine.

---

[19] parchment—long-lasting "paper" made out of animal skin.

[20] sheep and calves—fools.

[21] sirrah—like *sir*, but used for someone from a lower class than the speaker.

[22] *Wordplay:* Hamlet is making a pun. *Lie* means to tell a lie and to be in a place.

Hamlet. You lie in it when you are in it and say it is yours. A grave is for the dead, not for the quick.[23] Therefore, you lie.

First Gravedigger. It is a quick-moving lie, sir. It quickly goes from me to you.

Hamlet. What man do you dig it for?

First Gravedigger. For no man, sir.

Hamlet. What woman, then?

First Gravedigger. For none, neither.

Hamlet. Who is to be buried in it?

First Gravedigger. One that was a woman, sir, but, rest her soul, she's dead.

Hamlet. [*To* Horatio] How careful with his words the knave is! We must speak very correctly, or he will confuse us. By the Lord, Horatio, I have noticed in the last three years that common people today are as smart as educated men. [*To the* Gravedigger] How long have you been a gravedigger?

First Gravedigger. Of all the days in the year, I started the day that our last king Hamlet defeated Fortinbras in battle.

---

[23] quick—living. The gravedigger is also good at puns; see the next speech.

Hamlet. How long ago was that?

First Gravedigger. Don't you know that? Every fool knows that. It was the very day that young Hamlet was born—he that is mad and was sent to England.

Hamlet. Ay, marry, why was he sent into England?

First Gravedigger. Why, because he was mad. He shall get well there. Or, if he doesn't, it doesn't matter there.

Hamlet. Why?

First Gravedigger. They won't notice his madness there. In England the men are all as mad as he is.

Hamlet. How did he become mad?

First Gravedigger. Very strangely, they say.

Hamlet. How "strangely"?

First Gravedigger. Faith, he lost his sense.

Hamlet. Upon what ground?[24]

First Gravedigger. Why, here in Denmark. I have been a gravedigger here, man and boy, for thirty years.

---

[24] Upon what ground?—what are the reasons you judge that he is mad? *Wordplay: ground* can mean "reason" as well as "land, piece of earth." The gravedigger thinks Hamlet means "where."

Hamlet. How long will a man lie in the earth before he rots?

First Gravedigger. In faith, if he is not rotten before he dies—as we have many sick corpses now-a-days that will hardly hold together until they are buried—he will last about eight or nine years. A tanner[25] will last nine years.

Hamlet. Why will he last longer than the others?

First Gravedigger. Why, sir, his skin is so tanned in his job that he will keep out water a long time, and water is the worst decayer of a dead body. Here's a skull now. This skull has laid in the earth twenty-three years.

Hamlet. Whose was it?

First Gravedigger. A lowly mad fellow's it was. Whose do you think it was?

Hamlet. I don't know.

First Gravedigger. A sickness on him for a mad rogue! He poured a big glass of wine on my head once. This same skull, sir, was Yorick's skull, the king's jester.[26]

Hamlet. This?

---

[25] tanner—person who prepares leather to make it last longer.

[26] jester—comic; professional clown.

First Gravedigger. That.

Hamlet. Let me see. [Hamlet *takes the skull.*] Alas, poor Yorick! I knew him, Horatio—a fellow of infinite jest,[27] of most excellent imagination. He has carried me on his back a thousand times. And now, how terrible it is in my imagination! It almost makes me sick. Here hung those lips that I have kissed I don't know how often. Where are your jokes now? Your dances? Your songs? Your flashes of fun that made everyone at the table roar with laughter? Not one now to laugh at your own grinning? Are you quite sad now? Now, go to my lady's chamber and tell her that even though she paints her face an inch thick, she will end up looking like this. Make her laugh at that. I beg you, Horatio, tell me one thing.

Horatio. What's that, my lord?

Hamlet. Do you think Alexander[28] looked like this when he was buried?

Horatio. Just like that.

Hamlet. And smelled so? Pah!

[Hamlet *puts down the skull.*]

---

[27] infinite jest—unlimited jokes.

[28] Alexander the Great was the greatest conqueror Europeans knew from history. He was also very handsome. But death, of course, took both his empire and his physical beauty from him.

Horatio. Just like that, my lord.

Hamlet. To what low uses we may return when we die, Horatio! Why can't imagination trace the noble dust of Alexander until we find it stopping a hole in a beer barrel?

Horatio. It is too complicated to think that.

Hamlet. No, not a bit. It's easy to follow him there. Alexander died. Alexander was buried. Alexander returned to dust. The dust is earth. Of earth we make plaster, and why couldn't that plaster be used as a stopper in a beer-barrel?
Great Caesar, dead and turned to clay,
Might be used to fill a hole to keep the wind away.
O, that the earth he was made of, which kept the
    world in awe,
Should patch a wall to stop the winter's flaw.[29]
But wait! Wait! Here comes the king. [*Enter* Priest, *leading a funeral procession that includes the body of* Ophelia, Laertes, *and* King Claudius *and* Queen Gertrude *with their* Attendants.] The queen, the courtiers. Who is this they follow? And with so little ceremony? This must mean that the corpse they follow took its own life.

---

[29] *flaw*—gust of wind.

This was some high-born person. Let's hide here and watch.

[*They step aside.*]

Laertes. Why isn't there the proper ceremony?

Hamlet. That is Laertes, a very noble youth. Listen.

Laertes. Why isn't there the proper ceremony?

Priest. We are doing all we can. Her death was suspicious. She could not have been buried in a Christian graveyard if it weren't for the king's command. Yet here she is with her maiden garlands and flowers for the grave. And the bell is sounding for her.

Laertes. Is this all that will be done for her burial?

Priest. No more can be done. We would harm the service of the dead to sing a requiem[30] and give such rest to her as is given to souls who died at peace with God.

Laertes. Lay her in the earth. And from her fair and pure body may violets spring! I tell you, rude priest, my sister will be a caring angel when *you* lie howling in hell.

---

[30] requiem—music for a high Mass for the dead.

Hamlet. [*To* Horatio.] What, it's the fair Ophelia!

Queen Gertrude. Sweets to the sweet. Farewell! [*She scatters flowers in the grave.*] I hoped you would have been my Hamlet's wife. I thought I would prepare your bride-bed, sweet maid, and not have scattered flowers on your grave.

Hamlet. [*To* Horatio] What, the fair Ophelia?

Laertes. O, triple sorrow fall ten times triple on that cursed head of him whose wicked actions killed you! Do not cover her with earth until I have held her once more in my arms. [Laertes *leaps into the grave.*] Now pile the dirt upon the living and the dead until you have made a mountain, higher than the mountain the gods live on.

Hamlet. [*Joining the funeral*] Who is he whose grief is so strong, whose words of sorrow stop the movement of the stars and make them listen? It is I, Hamlet the Dane.

Laertes. [*Coming out of the grave*] The devil take your soul!

Hamlet. You don't pray very well. [Laertes *tries to strangle* Hamlet.] I pray you take your fingers off my throat. Though I am not hot tempered, yet I can be dangerous. Be careful. Take away your hand.

King Claudius. Pull them apart.

Queen Gertrude. Hamlet, Hamlet!

All. Gentlemen!

Horatio. [*To* Hamlet] Good my lord, be quiet.

[*The* Attendants *separate them.*]

Hamlet. Why, I will fight with him upon this theme until I'm dead.

Queen Gertrude. O my son, what theme?

Hamlet. I loved Ophelia. Forty thousand brothers could not, with all their love, care for her as much as I did. [*To* Laertes] What will you do for her?

King Claudius. O, he is mad, Laertes.

Queen Gertrude. For love of God, be patient with him.

Hamlet. God's wounds, show me what you'll do. Will you weep? Will you fight? Will you starve yourself? Will you tear at yourself? Will you drink vinegar? Eat a crocodile? I'll do it. Did you come here to whine? To do more than me by leaping in her grave? Be buried alive with her, and so will I. And, if you talk of mountains, let them throw millions of acres on us, until that mountain burns its head against the sun. It will

make the highest mountain look like a wart!
Nay, if you'll show off your sadness, I'll do it as
well as you.

Queen Gertrude. This is madness. Let him have
the fit. He will soon be quiet.

Hamlet. Hear me, sir. What is the reason that you
treat me like this? I have always been your
friend. But it doesn't matter. Let Hercules himself do what he may, the cat will mew and the
dog will have his day.[31]

[Hamlet *exits.*]

King Claudius. I pray you, good Horatio, look
after him. [*Exit* Horatio.] [*To* Laertes] Be patient,
and remember what I said to you last night. Our
plan will start now. Good Gertrude, send someone to look after your son. This grave shall have
a living monument.[32] We will have peace soon.
Until then, we must be patient.

[*They all exit.*]

---

[31] Hamlet says that just as a cat can't be kept quiet and a dog will be given his
chance, even if Hercules tries to stop them, he, Hamlet, will have his turn.

[32] The king will stand by the grave like a living monument. Or, the king will
build a monument that will last forever. Also, the king may be suggesting that
Hamlet will be killed as a monument for Ophelia.

ACT FIVE, SCENE TWO

In a hall in Elsinore castle, Hamlet tells Horatio how he
found out about the king's plot to kill him. Hamlet shows
Horatio the letter he wrote to replace the king's letter.
Instead of asking for Hamlet to be killed, the letter now
asks for the death of Rosencrantz and Guildenstern.
Hamlet agrees to fence with Laertes.

Hamlet is winning the fencing contest. Gertrude drinks
from the poisoned cup meant for Hamlet. Laertes then
wounds Hamlet with the poisoned sword point. Hamlet
grabs the sword and wounds Laertes. Gertrude dies.
Laertes, dying from the poison, confesses the plot to kill
Hamlet. Hamlet kills King Claudius, but before Hamlet
dies, he asks Horatio to tell the true story to everyone. He
says Fortinbras will be the next king of Denmark. After
Hamlet dies, Fortinbras arrives and restores order. He
orders a military funeral for Hamlet.

[*Enter* Hamlet *and* Horatio.]

Hamlet. So much for this, sir. Now I will tell you
the rest. You do remember what happened?

Horatio. Remember it, my lord!

Hamlet. Sir, in my heart there was a kind of fighting
That would not let me sleep. I thought
I was worse than a criminal in chains.
I did something rash without thinking about it.
Our hasty actions sometimes serve us well
When our deep plots fail. And that should
    teach us
There's a divinity that shapes our ends,
Rough-hew them how we will.[1]

Horatio. That is very true.

Hamlet. I came up from my cabin on the ship to
England. I stole the letter from King Claudius
that Rosencrantz and Guildenstern carried to
the king of England and returned to my room. I
opened the letter. I found, Horatio—a royal
wickedness! The letter ordered my death, giving
many reasons that were good for Denmark and

---

[1] Hamlet means that no matter how we plan our acts, God decides what will happen. These two famous lines are in Shakespeare's words.

England. As soon as the letter was read, without wasting time even to sharpen the ax, they should cut off my head.

Horatio. Is it possible?

Hamlet. Here's the letter. [*Handing him a paper.*] Read it when you have more time. But will you hear what I did then?

Horatio. I beg you to tell me.

Hamlet. Surrounded by villains, my brain came up with a plan before I could think about it. I sat down and wrote a new letter that looked very official. I once thought it a waste of time to learn to write that way, but, sir, now it did me a great service. Do you want to know what the letter said?

Horatio. Ay, good my lord.

Hamlet. I wrote an order from the king of Denmark. Since England was his faithful taxpayer, so that peace should stay between them, and many such important words, that, on the viewing and knowing of that letter, without further talk, he should put to sudden death the men who brought him this letter. He shouldn't even give them time to confess their sins.

Horatio. How did you seal the letter?[2]

Hamlet. Why, even in that, heaven helped me. I had my father's sealing ring in my pocket. It is the king's seal. I folded the letter up in the same way as the other, signed it, sealed it, and placed it safely back. No one ever knew I had changed it. Now, the next day was our sea fight. What happened there, you know already.

Horatio. So Guildenstern and Rosencrantz go to their death.

Hamlet. Why, man, they were part of this plan. They do not bother me. They destroyed themselves. It is dangerous for little men to get caught between two powerful men who are fighting.

Horatio. Why, what a king is this!

Hamlet. Don't you think that now it is my duty.— He that has killed my king, my father, and ruined my mother, taken the kingship away

---

[2] The king of Denmark would have sealed the letter with the royal seal pressed into hot wax.

from me, tried to have me killed, and with such tricks—isn't it perfectly right to pay him back with violence? And shouldn't I be damned if I let this spreading sore do more evil?

Horatio. He will soon know what happened in England.

Hamlet. It will be soon. I can use that time. And a man's life is very short. But I am very sorry, good Horatio, that I got angry with Laertes. For I can see why he believes I am to blame. I'll be his friend. But his bragging about his grief made me very angry.

Horatio. Peace! Who comes here?

[*Enter* Osric.]

Osric. [*Taking off his hat and repeatedly bowing*] Your lordship is very welcome back to Denmark.

Hamlet. I humbly thank you, sir. [*Aside to* Horatio] Do you know this waterfly?[3]

Horatio. No, my good lord.

---

[3] waterfly—insect with colored wings. Osric is dressed in bright colors.

Hamlet. You are blessed, for it is a pain to know him. He has much valuable land. He will be welcomed at court as long as he is rich.

Osric. [*Still bowing*] Sweet lord, if your lordship is at rest, I would tell a thing to you from his majesty.

Hamlet. I will receive it, sir, with all attention. Put your hat to its right use. It's for the head.

Osric. I thank your lordship. It is very hot.

Hamlet. No, believe me, it's very cold. The wind is northerly.

Osric. It is a little cold, my lord, indeed.

Hamlet. Yet I think it is very wet and too hot for me.

Osric. Exceedingly, my lord. It is very wet—I believe—I cannot tell how exactly. But, my lord, his majesty bade me signify[4] to you that he has laid a great wager on your head, sir. This is what happened—

[Osric *keeps bowing and waving his hat around.*]

---

[4] Osric is a showoff who wants to impress important people. He also likes to use big words. *Signify* means "tell" and *wager* means "bet."

Hamlet. I beg you, remember—

[Hamlet *signs to* Osric *to put on his hat.*]

Osric. No, my lord, for my ease, in good faith. Sir, Laertes has just returned to court from France. Believe me, he is a real gentleman, full of most excellent talents, with very pleasing manners and a distinguished appearance. Indeed, to speak feelingly of him, he is the card and calendar of gentry. He is a true gentleman.

Hamlet. Sir,[5] his definement suffers no perdition in you, though I know to divide him inventorially would dizzy the arithmetic of memory, and yet but yaw neither, in respect of his quick sail. But, in the verity of extolment, I take him to be a soul of great article; and his infusion of such dearth and rareness as, to make true diction of him, his semblable is his mirror, and who else would trace him, his umbrage, nothing more.

Osric. Your lordship speaks most infallibly[6] of him.

---

[5] In this speech Hamlet uses big words. The big words impress Osric. Shakespeare's audience didn't need to know what Hamlet was saying here. They knew he was making fun of Osric. Briefly, Hamlet is saying that Laertes is a great guy.

[6] infallibly—truthfully; without failing.

Hamlet. What are we saying, sir? Why are we using these words?

Osric. Sir?

Horatio. [*Aside to* Hamlet] Is it not possible to understand simpler words? You will do it, sir, really.

Hamlet. Why are you speaking about this gentleman?

Osric. Of Laertes?

Horatio. [*Aside*] His purse is empty already. All his golden words are spent.

Hamlet. About Laertes, sir.

Osric. I know you are not ignorant—

Hamlet. I wish you did, sir. Yet, in faith, if you did, it wouldn't matter much to me. Well, sir?

Osric. You are not ignorant of Laertes's excellence—

Hamlet. I dare not admit that, for then I would be saying that I am just as excellent, for a person cannot recognize what he doesn't have.

Osric. I mean, sir, for his weapon. He has the reputation of being the best in the use of his weapon.

Hamlet. What's his weapon?

Osric. Rapier and dagger.[7]

Hamlet. That's two of his weapons, but, well—

Osric. The king, sir, has bet six fine horses that in a fencing match between yourself and Laertes, he shall not exceed you by more than three hits. It would come to immediate trial, if your lordship would accept the challenge.

Hamlet. Sir, I will walk here in the hall. If it please his majesty, let the swords be brought. I will win for him if I can. If not, I will only have my shame and a few hits.

Osric. I commend[8] my duty to your lordship.

Hamlet. Yours. [Osric *exits.*] He does well to commend it to himself. No one else will commend him.

[*Enter a* Lord.]

---

[7] The rapier is a type of sword. The dagger is a short swordlike weapon used for stabbing.

[8] commend—offer; recommend.

Lord. My lord, his majesty sends me to ask if you will fence with Laertes now or later.

Hamlet. I will do as the king wishes. We can fence now or later. But I am ready if the king is ready.

Lord. The king and queen and all are coming down.

Hamlet. They are welcome.

Lord. The queen desires you to greet Laertes in a friendly way before you begin the sport.

Hamlet. She gives me good advice.

[*Exit* Lord.]

Horatio. You will lose this bet, my lord.

Hamlet. I do not think so. Since he went to France, I have practiced a great deal. I shall do well enough. However, I don't feel good about this. But it is no matter.

Horatio. No, wait, my lord—

Hamlet. It is foolish to feel this way. It is a feeling that might trouble a woman.[9]

---

[9] Hamlet is getting a *premonition*, a warning feeling that something bad will happen. But he tries to dismiss it as being unmanly to feel this way.

Horatio. If you think you shouldn't do this, don't do it. I will stop them from coming here and say you are not feeling well.

Hamlet. No, we will fight against these fears about the future. There's a special reason for the fall of even a sparrow.[10] If death happens now, it will not happen in the future. If it will not happen in the future, it will happen now. If it doesn't happen now, it will still happen sometime. Being ready is everything. Since no man can know what he will miss when he is gone, what does it matter if he dies early?

[*Enter* King Claudius, Queen Gertrude, Laertes, Lords, Osric, *and* Attendants *with swords.*]

King Claudius. Come, Hamlet, come, and shake hands with Laertes.

[King Claudius *puts Laertes's hand into Hamlet's.*]

Hamlet. Forgive me, sir. I've done you wrong.
But forgive me, as you are a gentleman.
    Everyone here knows,
And you must have heard, how my mind is suffering.

---

[10] Hamlet is referring to the Bible. "Fear not, therefore, you are more valuable than many sparrows." Matthew 10:29–31.

What I have done that has harmed you or
    your honor,
I here say was madness.
Did Hamlet wrong Laertes? Never Hamlet.
If Hamlet is not himself,
And when he's not himself wrongs Laertes,
Then Hamlet doesn't do it. Hamlet denies it.
Who does it, then? His madness. If it be so,
Hamlet is also wronged. His madness is poor
    Hamlet's enemy.
Please believe that I did not plan to harm you.

Laertes. My personal feelings are satisfied, but you have wronged my father. Someone will have to show me how in the past others have forgiven such an action. Until that time, I accept your offer of friendship like a friend and will not harm it.

Hamlet. I welcome you like a brother. And we will play this game of fencing like honest brothers. Give us the foils.[11] Come on.

Laertes. Come, one for me.

Hamlet. I'll be your foil, Laertes. My lack of skill will make your skill shine like a star in the dark night.

---

[11] foils—swords often used for sport fighting. *Wordplay:* Hamlet next uses *foil* to mean something shiny, like aluminum foil, that reflects the light of a jewel.

Laertes. You mock me, sir.

Hamlet. No, I swear it.

King Claudius. Give them the foils, young Osric. Cousin Hamlet, you know the bet?

Hamlet. Very well, my lord. Your grace has backed the weaker side.

King Claudius. I'm not afraid. I have seen you both. But, since he is better, he has to hit you three more times.

Laertes. [*Holding a sword*] This is too heavy. Let me see another.

Hamlet. I like this one. Are all these foils the same length?

[*They prepare to fight.*]

Osric. Yes, my good lord.

King Claudius. Set the cups of wine on that table. If Hamlet gives the first or second hit, let all the cannons be fired. We shall all drink to Hamlet. And I will throw a pearl into Hamlet's cup, richer than any that the last four kings in Denmark have worn in their crown. Give me the cups. Play the trumpets, sound the drums. Now the king drinks to Hamlet. Come, begin. And you, the judges, watch carefully.

[*Trumpets play.*]

Hamlet. Come on, sir.

Laertes. Come, my lord.

[*They fight.*]

Hamlet. One.[12]

Laertes. No.

Hamlet. Judgment!

Osric. A hit, a very palpable[13] hit.

Laertes. Very well. Let's go again.

King Claudius. Wait. Give me a drink. Hamlet, this pearl is yours. Here's to your health. [*He drinks, then drops the pearl in the cup.*] [*Drums, trumpets, and cannon sound.*] Give him the cup.[14]

Hamlet. I'll play this bout first. Set it down awhile. Come. [*They fight.*] Another hit. Do you agree?

---

[12] One—Hamlet has touched Laertes with the tip of his sword. This would give Hamlet a point in the match.

[13] palpable—obvious. Osric won't give up his long words.

[14] Claudius is trying to get Hamlet to drink the poisoned wine.

Laertes. A touch, a touch, I do confess.

King Claudius. Our son shall win.

Queen Gertrude. He's out of shape and breathing hard. Here, Hamlet, take my handkerchief, rub your face. The queen drinks to your fortune, Hamlet.

[*She lifts the cup.*]

Hamlet. Good madam.

King Claudius. [*Panicked*] Gertrude, do not drink.

Queen Gertrude. I will, my lord. I pray you, pardon me.

[*She drinks and offers the cup to* Hamlet.]

King Claudius. [*Aside*] It is the poisoned cup. It is too late.

Hamlet. I dare not drink yet, madam. Soon.

Queen Gertrude. Come, let me wipe your face.

Laertes. [*To* Claudius] My lord, I'll hit him now.

King Claudius. I do not think so.

Laertes. [*Aside*] And yet it's almost against my conscience.

Hamlet. Come, for the third time, Laertes. You are holding back. I pray you, try your best. I fear you are making a fool of me.

Laertes. Do you say that? Come on.

[*They fight.*]

Osric. Nothing, neither way.

Laertes. Have at you now!

[Laertes *wounds* Hamlet. *Then, in real fighting, they exchange swords, and* Hamlet *wounds* Laertes.][15]

King Claudius. Part them. They have lost their tempers.

Hamlet. No, come again.

[Queen Gertrude *falls.*]

Osric. Look to the queen there!

Horatio. They are both bleeding. How are you, my lord?

Osric. How are you, Laertes?

Laertes. Why, as a bird caught in my own trap, Osric. [*He falls.*] I am justly killed by my own treachery.

---

[15] What takes so little space here would be a very dramatic sword fight on stage.

Hamlet. How is the queen?

King Claudius. She faints to see you bleed.

Queen Gertrude. No, no, the drink, the drink!
O my dear Hamlet! The drink, the drink! I
am poisoned.

[*She dies.*]

Hamlet. O villainy! Lock the door!

[Osric *exits.*]

Treachery! Find the traitor.

Laertes. It is here, Hamlet. Hamlet, you are killed.
No medicine in the world can save you.
You will not live for half an hour.
The treacherous weapon is in your hand.
Sharp and poisoned. My evil trick
Has turned against me. See, here I lie,
Never to rise again. Your mother's poisoned.
I can't go on. The king, the king's to blame.

Hamlet. The point!—Poisoned too! Then, poison,
do your work.

[Hamlet *stabs* King Claudius *with the poisoned sword.*]

All. Treason! treason!

King Claudius. O, yet defend me, friends. I am only hurt.

Hamlet. Here, you incestuous, murderous, damned Dane, drink this poison. Follow my mother.

[Hamlet *forces the* king *to drink from the cup with poison.* King Claudius *dies.*]

Laertes. He deserved that. It is a poison he made. Exchange forgiveness with me, noble Hamlet. Mine and my father's death are not your fault. Nor is your death my fault.

[Laertes *dies.*]

Hamlet. Heaven forgive you! I follow you.
I am dying, Horatio.—Wretched queen, adieu!—
You who look pale and tremble at what has
    happened,
Who cannot speak, the audience for this act,
If I had time—but this cruel officer, Death,
Is strict in his arrest—O, I could tell you—
But let it be. Horatio, I am dying.
You live. Truly tell those who do not know
What I did and why.

Horatio. Never believe it. I am more like an ancient Roman than a Dane.[16] Here's some liquor left. [*He picks up the cup.*]

Hamlet. As you are a man, give me the cup. Let go. By heaven, I'll have it.

O God, Horatio, what evil people will think of me when I die.

If you ever thought of me as your friend,

Keep yourself from the happiness of death for a while,

And in this harsh world draw your breath in pain

To tell my story.

[*A march is played far off, and shots are fired.*]

What warlike noise is this?

[Osric *enters.*]

Osric. Young Fortinbras is back from defeating Poland and has saluted our ambassadors returning from England.

Hamlet. O, I die, Horatio!

The powerful poison overcomes me.

I cannot live to hear the news from England.

---

[16] Horatio, like the ancient Romans, will die with his friend.

But I predict Fortinbras will be the next
King of Denmark. He has my dying vote.
So tell him what has happened, more or less.
The rest is silence.

[Hamlet *dies.*]

Horatio. Now cracks a noble heart. Good night,
sweet prince,
And flights of angels sing you to your rest!
[*The sounds of military drums are heard.*]
Why does the drum come here?
[*Marching is heard offstage. Enter* Fortinbras, *the*
English Ambassador, *and* Soldiers.]

Prince Fortinbras. What has happened?

Horatio. What is it you would see? If you seek sorrow or disaster, stop searching.

Prince Fortinbras. Why are so many dead? O
proud death, what feast are you having that you
have struck down so many?

English Ambassador. This is a terrible sight! And
we have come from England too late. The king is
dead. We would have told him his orders have
been carried out, that Rosencrantz and
Guildenstern are dead. Who will thank us for this?

Horatio. Not him, even if he were alive to
  thank you.

  He never ordered their death.

  But since you have arrived at the right
  moment,

  [*To* Fortinbras] you from the war in Poland, and

  [*To the* English Ambassador] you from England,

  Give orders that these bodies be placed on a
  high platform

  Where everyone can see them.

  Let me tell how these things happened.

  You will hear of sinful, bloody, and
  unnatural acts,

  Of accidental judgments, chance murders,

  Of deaths caused by cunning and trickery.

  And, finally, misunderstood actions

  Falling on the inventors' heads.

  All this I can truly say.

Prince Fortinbras. Quickly tell us. And call the
  noblest to hear. For me, with sorrow I embrace
  my fate. I have some claim in this kingdom.
  And this seems to be the time to make my claim.

Horatio. I shall also speak of that. Hamlet spoke
  for you, and I will speak for him. But let me
  speak immediately. We must tell the truth before
  any more plots and misunderstandings happen.

Prince Fortinbras. Let four captains

Carry Hamlet like a soldier to the platform,

For he was likely, had he been tested,

To have proved to be a great king. And, to
mark his death,

Play the soldiers' music and bury him as a
soldier.

Take up the bodies. Such a sight as this

Is right for the battlefield, but does not
belong here.

Go, command the soldiers

To fire shots as a salute to these deaths.

[*A military funeral march is played. The stage is cleared. The dead bodies are carried off. Then, as is the custom at a military funeral, even today, a round of gun shots is fired as a salute.*]